£18

Be

THE ART AND LIFE OF FATHER SOPHRONY

2nd edition

SISTER GABRIELA

STAVROPEGIC MONASTERY OF ST. JOHN THE BAPTIST · ESSEX ·

BEING
The art and life of Father Sophrony
by Sister Gabriela

First edition 2016
ISBN 978-1-909649-07-1

Second (paperback) edition 2019
ISBN 978-1-909649-20-0

Illustrations: All material reproduced in this book comes from private archives and is covered by copyright.

All photographs by the Stavropegic Monastery of St John the Baptist except where otherwise stated

Design by MikeStonelake.com

Published by the Stavropegic Monastery of St John the Baptist, Tolleshunt Knights, by Maldon, Essex CM9 8EZ, UK

Contents

Introduction

THIS BOOK CAME TO be for two reasons.

After the publication of *Seeking Perfection in the World of Art,*[1] some material was found showing that Archimandrite Sophrony,[2] then known as Sergei Sakharov, was one of the founding members of the art group 'Bytie' (being). This fact which so mirrored his lifelong search for the meaning and reason of *being/Being* inspired the idea to make a special study of this particular aspect of his life.

The chapters develop by treating the various periods of his life, starting with his time in Russia as a painter, followed by his struggle to express eternity in his art and his existential searches, which lead him to oriental religions. In chapter 3 he finds his way back to Christianity and turns to the monastic life. Finally in chapter 4 he returns to painting, but this time in the form of icons, expressing in visual form the fruit of his labour and much tried ascetic experience.

As I am a painter, the theological aspects have only been touched upon very briefly. It is my hope that others will develop these aspects further and deeper in future.

The second reason for this book was that it gave me the opportunity to publish some of Father Sophrony's further thoughts on Orthodox icon painting, which I had not been able to include in the first book. I learned to know him while still a teenager. He inspired me to study

1. Sister Gabriela, *Seeking Perfection in the World of Art,* Tolleshunt Knights: Stavropegic Monastery of Saint John the Baptist, 2016.
2. *Archimandrite* is the official ecclesiastical title of Father Sophrony within the Orthodox Church; however we have chosen to refer to him in the simpler formula of *Father.*

icon painting and when I joined his monastery at the age of twenty, I was included in the group of painters. During the next ten years I assisted him in several artistic projects, which is when I took the notes included here. Having inherited much from him during that time, I was looking for a way to share both his teaching and reflection on iconography.[3] It must be said in his defense that I was still very young and his explanations were directed to a child; he would have spoken differently to a more mature person. Also, Father Sophrony always respected each person, independent of age or gender, and valued their freedom above a set idea or concept, if he met with resistance – either voluntary or through ignorance – he would defer to the other. Therefore, any mistakes in this book are entirely my own where I may have misunderstood what he meant and Father Sophrony can in no way be held responsible. He always encouraged me to study further, as the icon is linked to eternity and the end is not attainable in this life: *Prepare yourself spiritually for the painting of icons and be ruthless with yourself: don't sleep, be very attentive, pray more and at the same time be cheerful. Try to accomplish all this at the same time!*

3. Throughout this book the term 'iconographic' is used in the Christian Orthodox meaning, as a synonym to 'sacred art', not in the current art-historical meaning, denoting any image.

CHAPTER 1

In the Search for *Being*

> THE HUMAN SPIRIT HUNGERS for knowledge – for entire, integral knowledge … of Primordial Being, of Whom or What actually exists.[4]

The quest for knowledge of *being* runs like a thread throughout Father Sophrony's life. At times it gets very fragile, in danger of snapping, at other times it wears tenuously thin; but in spite of all the tribulations, it is not broken and through tireless perseverance it ends up not just as a strong rope, but ultimately, a lifeline.

Sergei Simeonovich Sakharov (1896-1993), the future Father Sophrony, was from early childhood preoccupied with the question of eternity. He would discuss and speculate with his friends in the earnest manner of young children about where their grandparents and other people who had died would be. As he was raised in a practicing Orthodox Christian family, he was taught to pray for the departed, but this did not satisfy his curiosity. The Sakharov family was a large one. Sergei had nine siblings, of whom he was the third oldest until the age of 13 when his elder brother by one year died leaving Sergei the oldest son of the family. Their mother, Ekaterina Evgen'evna, was a deeply believing woman and was concerned that her children were given a religious upbringing. The children were mainly cared for by a nanny, who was a pious and prayerful woman. She would often take Sergei with her to church services and he would be accustomed to spend many long hours sitting at her feet praying. It was coming out from the Church on such occasions that he was sometimes given to see Moscow not only in the natural light of day but bathed in an otherworldly golden light while

4. A. Sophrony, *His Life is Mine*, Crestwood: Saint Vladimir's Seminary Press, 1988, p. 17.

at the same time feeling an ineffable joy and peace. He often had this spiritual experience but it was only much later in life that he realized the gift of these manifestations of light.[5]

However, Sergei had a normal childhood, he loved to have fun with his friends and was a passionate football player. Once in winter, he and his friends climbed up onto the top of a shed in the courtyard but accidentally they slipped and slid from the roof with a free-fall down into a large snowdrift, which providentially was just underneath. They immediately set out to repeat the action and would have done so, if a grown up had not stopped them. Later, as an artist, Sergei would again take walks on the roof of the house of his studio, high up above Moscow, in order to clear his thoughts.

Simeon Sakharov, the father of the family, was a manufacturer of superior quality ladies' handbags. He was patronized by the distinguished society of Moscow. He was friends with one of Moscow's leading tailors[6] who supplied him with suits and consequently he was always most elegantly well dressed. He was a handsome man and at the same time warm hearted. He liked to be merry and to joke. He arranged for his children to attend the best schools, providing a solid education, rich in Russian literature and culture. While it is not known for certain which Moscow school Sergei attended as a boy, it is likely to have been a classical *gymnasium*, where he would have studied sacred history and elements of Christian doctrine, Russian and European literature, both classical languages and French, secular history, calligraphy and a number of other disciplines — staples of normal education in the Russian Empire. During his adolescence, Sergei would also frequently visit the opera and listen to Chaliapin, whom he admired.

---

5. A. Sophrony, unpublished letter.
6. It is not sure who this tailor was, possibly K. I. Dellos, who was considered to be one of Moscow's ten best tailors and whose shop on the Sretenskiy Boulevard was not far from the house of the Sakharov family. (http://www.raruss.ru/russe-moderne/3971-aleshina-russian-modern-clothes.html)

Once writing to his sister, he referred to an occasion when he and his father were both sitting at the table in the hall reading; the father was reading a newspaper while Sergei read Turgenev. He asked his father why he read newspapers and not better literature, whereupon his father answered that as he himself was interested in history, the newspaper was tomorrow's history. Sergei was not convinced.[7] The family generally avoided high-flown language and superficial eloquence, as 'fancy talk' was considered indecent.

The Sakharov children were also taught to appreciate art. The family owned an original landscape painting that hung in the salon. They were forced to sell this painting during the years of starvation. For Sergei, whose passion was art, the disappearance of the painting was felt as the loss of a family member. From his very young years he would often sit under the table in the hall drawing. His father was an accomplished draughtsman and particularly good at drawing horses, which spurred young Sergei also to master their difficult anatomy and movement. The schools provided some basic art training, but Sergei would have previously enrolled in an evening art class to prepare for the entrance exam to the Moscow Institute of Painting, Sculpture and Architecture, the Moscow equivalent of the St Petersburg Academy of Art, the ambition for any aspiring artist. Judging by his later technical skills and style, the studio he most probably attended was that of Fedor Rerberg, which provided a sound, classical foundation in all the traditional techniques of art. The atelier of Viktor Vasnetsov was just a block away from the family home and may well have been another place that Sergei frequented. He held this painter in deep respect, considering him to be a patriarch among the painters, whose 'blessing' he made it a point to obtain before leaving Russia.

7. A. Sophrony, *Letters to his Family*, Tolleshunt Knights: Stavropegic Monastery of St. John the Baptist, 2015, p. 278.

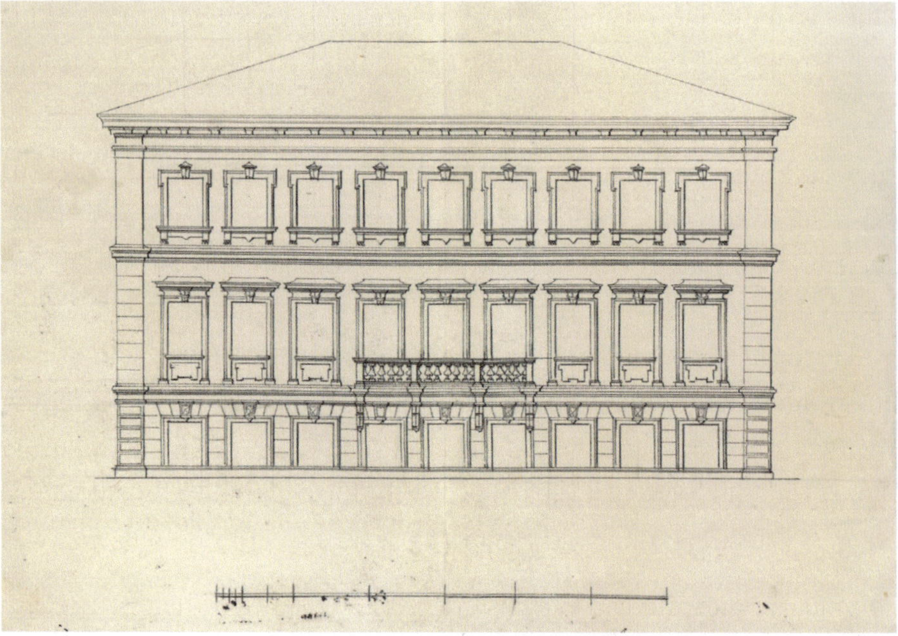

The Sakharov family house, 1868,

2nd Meshanskaia street, house 2, 3rd floor, flat 23.
(TSGA Moscow, OKhTDM, fond 1, op. 6, d. 316)

Sergei was born in 1896, during the reign of Nicholas II, the twilight of the Russian empire. The first eight years of his childhood were a time of peace up until the outbreak of the war with Japan after which his life coincided with the most tragic cataclysmic events.

> I was still a young man when the tragedy of historical events far outdid anything that I had read in books. (I refer to the outbreak of the First World War, soon to be followed by the Revolution in Russia.) My youthful hopes and dreams collapsed.[8]

In 1905 the first revolution occurred in Russia followed in 1914 by the outbreak of World War 1 and then in 1917, the revolution and coup d'état of the Bolsheviks resulted in the civil war. All these tragic circumstances only strengthened Sergei's existential questions: why was he born and what was the purpose of life if it was all to end in death and eternal oblivion. These questions tormented him to a degree that he felt himself on the brink of insanity. He did not reveal his inner turmoil to anyone and outwardly continued to live and behave as any other young man, often laughing and joking, yet, the question kept burning within him. Because of his inner struggle, he did not get deeply involved with other young people and searched for a solution in his art.

Figurative art, being free from the constraints of time, lends itself to the expression and search for the eternal. The exploration of how best to represent the infinite and timeless was a trend developed especially by the symbolist artists at the beginning of the 20th century in Russia, the so-called *Silver Age*. Sergei was not actively involved in any group, but was open-minded, studying all previous attempts to find answers to his existential questions and searching for a solution on his own.

---

8. *His Life is Mine*, p. 38.

The question of death became acute, as did the concept of eternal oblivion; *non-being*. "I contemplated death not only in the body, in death's terrestrial forms, but in eternity."[9]

In spite of his inner turmoil he continued to pray, as he had been taught in childhood by his nanny. He also read the gospels, but did not understand much of them, just clinging to them in the way he had been taught as a child, until one day, at the age of 17, when walking down a street in Moscow, the thought in the form of a doubt suddenly hit him. The thought told him that the gospel teaching of love was just psychological, and with a conscious effort he stopped himself praying.

He then turned to eastern religions, meditation and yoga, trying through these practices to come to know the unknowable and unattainable, the mystery of *being*. It was a trend among the artists, especially of the Silver Age, to explore all types of esoteric practices and movements.

> His studio was at the top of a tall house in a quiet part of Moscow. There he would labour for hours on end, straining every nerve to depict his subject dispassionately, to convey its temporal significance, yet at the same time to use it as a spring-board for exploring the infinite. He was tortured by conflicting arguments: if life was generated by the eternal, why did his body need to breathe, eat, sleep, and so on? Why did it react to every variation in the physical atmosphere? In an effort to break out of the narrow framework of existence he took up yoga and applied himself to meditation. But he never lost his keen awareness of the beauty of nature.
>
> Daily life now flowed on the periphery, as it were, of external events. The one thing needful was to discover the purport of

9. A. Sophrony, *We Shall See Him As He Is*, Tolleshunt Knights: Stavropegic Monastery of Saint John the Baptist, 1988, p. 13.

> our appearance on this planet; to revert to the moment before creation and be merged with our original source. He continued oblivious to social and political affairs – utterly preoccupied by the thought that if man dies without the possibility of returning to the sphere of Absolute Being, then life held no meaning. Occasionally, meditation would bring respite with an illusion of some unending quietude which had been his fountain-head.[10]

Sergei ardently studied the philosophical artistic thinkers of the time, trying to find a solution. From these, the person who had the strongest impact on him was Wassily Kandinsky.

KANDINSKY, PURE CREATIVITY

> In my young days, through a Russian painter who afterwards became famous, I had been attracted to the idea of pure creativity, taking the form of abstract art.[11]

The concept of pure creativity answered Sergei's longing and search to portray the unattainable and the infinite. Abstract painting was or seemed to be the best way to convey the inexpressible and intangible with visions of another new creation.

Kandinsky, though not resident in Russia until 1915,[12] was still already well known in his homeland. He had been returning every summer and had participated in several exhibitions. In 1915 his abstract painting, Composition VII was exhibited in Moscow at the Art Salon on the Bolshaia Dmitrovka. This was the first time his abstract work was shown in Russia. His book, "On the Spiritual in Art", had been presented at the Pan-Russian Congress of Artists in St. Petersburg already in 1911 and

10. R. Edmonds, Introduction, *A. Sophrony*, His Life is Mine, pp. 7-8.
11. A. Sophrony, Wisdom from Mount Athos, Crestwood: St. Vladimir's Seminary Press, 1974, p. 13.
12. Kandinsky, had been forced to leave Germany with the outbreak of WWI.

it appeared in print in Russian in 1915.[13] This coincided with the time that Sergei himself was searching for answers to his spiritual questions through art to some of which Kandinsky had already found solutions: "Painting is an art. Art is not the senseless creation of things, diffused in a vacuum. It is a powerful force and has many aims. It should serve the development and refinement of the human soul."[14] "When the soul is neglected and suffocated, by mere pragmatic aspirations, then people believe that art is given to man for no particular purpose – that it has no aim, that it exists only for itself." [15]

In raising the sphere of art to serve the development of the soul, Kandinsky lifted the whole concept to another level. Art became a path to explore and solve the meaning of *being*.

> A creative work is born from the artist in a very mysterious, enigmatic and mystical manner. Liberated from him, it takes on its own independent, spiritual being which also leads a material and concrete life, it is a *being*. Consequently, this is not an accidental phenomenon, indifferent and insensitive to spiritual life. But, like any being, it is a phenomenon which possesses its own creative, active forces. It lives, acts and participates in the creation of the spiritual atmosphere….[16]

Kandinsky laid great emphasis on the necessity of inner freedom to be able to create 'pure art'. The artist should posses and cultivate his inner life, from which the forms of new creation were to spring, expressing the artist's inner dreams in his own uniquely constructed lines, shapes

13. Sergei would have read *On the Spiritual in Art* early on and been very influenced by it; throughout his later writings some of his expressions and images seem to be very similar to the ones used by Kandinsky.
14. V. Kandinsky, *On the Spiritual in Art (1920)*, Experiment Vol. 8, Los Angeles, 2002, p. 113.
15. J. E. Bowlt and R. C. Washton Long, *The Life of Vasilii Kandinsky in Russian Art, a study of On the Spiritual in Art*, Newtonville, Mass.: Oriental Research Partners, 1980, p. 99.
16. *The Life of Vasilii Kandinsky*, p. 98.

and colours.[17] The expression of the artist should emerge from an inner vibration. This vibration could be influenced or inspired by observing nature, but it was of primary importance that it was free and not conditioned by any laws, constraints or intellectual limitations.[18]

Sergei worked ardently to realize the solution in his art, searching for inner resonances in relation to the world around him.

> Just as every artist apprehends objective reality through the forms and modes of his art, so I derived ideas for my abstract studies from life around me. I would look at a man, a house, a plant, at intricate machinery, extravagant shadowscapes on walls or ceilings, at quivering bonfire flames, and would compose them into abstract pictures, creating in my imagination visions that were not like actual reality, this was how I interpreted the teaching of my master – not to copy natural phenomena but to produce new pictorial facts.[19]

Inspired by Kandinsky's thought, Sergei would do large studies and compositional improvisations. Kandinsky expressed his method in a letter written in 1915: "I am working a lot in watercolor. It is very precise work and I am, so to speak, learning the art of the jeweler. It helps me prepare for the large paintings, which are slowly taking shape in my heart."[20] Kandinsky specially emphasized the need for exercises in composition because these cultivated the ability to create, appreciating the value of artistic logical analysis as well as nurturing criticism and feelings of inner freedom.[21] Each colour

---

17. Cf. Kandinksy *Complete Writings on Art*, translated and edited by K.C. Lindsay and Peter Vergo, Boston, USA: Da Capo, 1994, pp. 414-416.
18. 18. Cf. *The Life of Vasilii Kandinsky*, pp. 79, 81.
19. *Wisdom*, p. 13.
20. Vivian Endicott Barnett, *Kandinsky Watrcolours and Drawings*. Munich: Prestel Verlag, 1992. p. 36.
21. Cf. Wassily Kandinsky, *Unterricht am Bauhaus 1923-1933*, ed. A. Weißbach, Gebr Mann Verlag, Berlin, 2015, p. 239.

> and shape had its own movement, 'temperature' and direction. It was essential to find "the right scale, for the exact missing weight, the way in which the left scale trembles at the merest touch on the right, the tiniest alternations of drawing and color in such a place that the whole picture is made to vibrate…",[22] in this way to create graphic 'counterpoint'.[23] Another goal was to summarize the harmonious effect which was achieved through organization of parallel and opposite movements. These elements were to be built up into complex forms and combinations, while juxtaposed between pointed and rounded shapes, which in their turn equaled warm and cold. [24]

During his studies, Sergei had the use of the scenic decoration workshop of the Bolshoi Theatre which was only a few blocks away from the school. The vast space available was situated just under the roof of the large theatre and provided unlimited freedom and scope for Sergei, especially since at the time there were not many productions staged there.[25] Hidden out of sight, it gave opportunity to experiment on a larger scale, working on canvases of unrestricted size.

His work was interrupted by repeated periods of military service under the rapidly changing political 'flags'.[26] He received the full military training, being especially gifted at target shooting. He was however never sent to the front and was grateful that he was not required to use his gift as a crack-shot. At the same time he did not entirely lose

22. *Complete Writings*, p. 387.
23. Cf. *The Life of Vasilii Kandinsky*, pp. 80-81.
24. Cf. *Unterricht*, pp. 257-277.
25. In the first years after the Revolution there was much discussion about whether the theatre should be closed as it had strong links with the former regime. Eventually the decision was taken to keep it open and before long the theatre was back in full use with its full repertoire. In 1921 the building was closed for major restoration work and reopened again in 1922.
26. Soon after elementary school Sergei was drafted into the Tsarist army. During the provisional government in 1917 he again served in the army, this time under Kerensky. With the Bolsheviks rise to power he was called up once more, on this occasion into the Red army.

valuable painting time while doing his military service, since as a junior officer in the engineering department he was placed in the newly formed camouflage division. A delegation from the Russian army had visited the camouflage workshops in Paris in 1916 to learn the techniques, and the post-revolution Soviet army continued to develop this craft. Clearly the time in the army designing camouflage was profitable for Sergei, because he learned new techniques in the fragmenting of images to create an abstract design.

Kandinsky's old friend Franz Marc[27] was at the time working in the camouflage division of the opposite camp and in 1916 wrote to his wife:

> I was standing in a huge hay barn (a beautiful atelier!) and painted 9 'Kandinskys' ... on military tent canvases. The thing is harmless, - the 'art' was in this case luckily switched off ... I have had strange sensations while doing it. The aim is totally utilitarian, being to cover constructions with canvases in order not to be seen from the air and recognized in aerial photography. These canvases are painted according to a rough pointillist system using the knowledge of bright natural colours (mimicry). The distance is enormous, on average 2000m high, ... The result is that the countryside is obscured to such an extent that the location is unidentifiable... I am curious to see how the Kandinskys look at 2000 m. The 9 canvases show a development 'from Monet to Kandinsky'! [28]

The same camouflage techniques as well as aerial photography were used by the Russian army. The aerial photographs inspired artists such as Malevich which bore expression in his personal style of suprematism. As the camouflage technique had a strong resemblance to Kandinsky's work, Sergei could to a certain extent continue his quest while still in

27. Franz Marc (1880-1916), painter and friend of Kandinsky.
28. Franz Marc, *Briefe aus dem Feld,* München: R. Piper & Co. Verlag, 1982, p. 141, (6. II. 1916).

The Svomas/VKhUTEMAS building, 1920's,
Moscow, Miasnitskaia Street.

Moscow, Miasnitskaia Street, 1920's.

the army. Another vital part of the training in camouflage was the aspect of breaking up a surface or colour into smaller fragments or lines of pure colour. These would be juxtaposed in order to create the semblance of blended colours from a distance. The dissecting and analysis of colour and shape in this way, which would not have come naturally to an art student in normal conditions, was of great advantage to Sergei. He learned how to create vibrating surfaces and how to dissimulate and model his subjects as needed. This was helpful on a practical level, but he felt that he was losing valuable time in developing a method of painting, which would have the potential to depict the eternal. The urgency of solving the question of *being* was intensified by the daily horrifying reports of casualties from the front.

BENATOV

In-between Sergei's various periods in military service, he enrolled in the studio of Il'ia Mashkov, which specialized in preparing students for the exacting entrance exams for the Moscow Institute of Painting. Here he found a like-minded young man, Leonardo Benatov,who was to become a lifelong and important friend to Sergei. Leon (Levon) Mikhailovich Bounatian (1899-1972) (later know as Leonardo Benatov[29]) was born in Kağızman in the district of Yerevan in Armenia, which at the time was under Russian rule. He was from a princely family, but Benatov preferred to hide this fact, arguing that titles should be endowed in response to one's achievements, not from birth. Though of Armenian descent, the family belonged to the Orthodox faith and the children, Leonardo and his three sisters, were given a pious upbringing. In 1909 his family moved to Tibilisi where Leonardo attended evening classes in an art school modeled on the Moscow School of Painting. To pursue a more serious art education,

---

29. His name was changed to this when he emigrated and registered in France, due to a misspelling. In order to be consistent throughout this book, his 'French' name shall be used in the texts, except where there is a quote from a contemporary source.

P. Konchalovsky, *Portait of Leonardo Benatov*, 1920.
Photograph courtesy of Sotheby's.

he moved to Moscow in 1915, where he at first enrolled in the studio of Milman and Miganadjiyan, but in 1916 changed to the studio of Mashkov. This is when he met Sergei. From their very first contact they discovered that they shared a common striving: to try to attain and express the eternal in art and to attain the mystery of *being*.

Together they explored various spiritual paths, sharing their experiences and dreams. Benatov found lodgings in a nearby street to Sergei's house and became like a member of the Sakharov family.

During the year 1917, when the art schools mostly stopped functioning due to the political unrest and civil strife, Benatov shared a studio on Nikolskaya street with Aleksandr and I. F.Smirnov, who had been his teacher at the studio of Miganadjiyan. Through his acquaintance with Rodchenko, Benatov discovered abstract art and started drawing circles and colouring them in under a spectrum. He was also interested in cubism, but it was Rodchenko's constructivism that attracted him more strongly. Rodchenko himself was in a period of transition; it would only be four years later that he was to abandon painting altogether for constructive design, sculpture and, later, photography. It is likely that Sergei also came to know him at this time.

As mentioned above, 1917 was a year of extreme instability. Sergei was drafted into the army, then led by Kerensky, but fortunately was not put in a fighting position but rather assigned to the 6th school of warrant officers.[30]

Although he was not involved in direct fighting, the acute situation only intensified Sergei's inner suffering, bringing him to the brink of despair.

> I was living as if in a dream. And that dream was a nightmare…. at times a dark abyss opened under me and a thick leaden wall was looming over me. I was twice arrested at the beginning of the

30. This section included the division of engineers who were in charge of camouflage. At the time, Konchalovsky, who had been his teacher at the Mashkov studio, was teaching at the military school of camouflage. It is possible that Sergei was one of his pupils there.

> revolution. Many people perished at the time but I felt no fear, as if there were nothing terrible in those arrests. But the vision of that wall and that abyss put me in a state of inexplicable, silent terror. And this went on for many years. [31]

Sergei's anguish was so great that the danger of execution, which was a reality during his arrests, paled in front of his inner torments. He did not adhere to any political party, as none of them offered a solution to his agony. At the time of the October events, the coup d'état of the Bolsheviks, Sergei was spared from being forced to take any sides, as he was ill with typhus which was epidemic and, together with the general state of deprivation and starvation, took many lives. Sergei, however, was spared.

In 1918, when life had come back to some kind of normality and stability, he and Benatov became members of the Professional Association of Artists. This was the first attempt after the Revolution to unite all types of painters, but it ceased to function as early as 1919 due to inner tensions and divisions. During its brief existence, the two friends attached themselves, as abstract artists, to the left faction. It was during these internal clashes, in which their teacher Mashkov was spokesman for the central faction, that Benatov found himself in the dilemma of being divided in sympathies, but finally he made the decision to adhere to figurative art, joining the position of Mashkov in the central faction.

For Sergei, the decision to move away from abstract art was more from his dissatisfaction with its possibilities, compounded by his growing despair which will be examined further in the next chapter.

In the summer of 1918, the two friends decided that they were ready to apply for entrance into the renowned Moscow Institute of Painting, Sculpture and Architecture. However the time of their applications coincided with the school being transformed into a more suitable form

---

31. A. Sophrony, *Tainstvo khristianskoi zhizni,* Sergiev Posad: Sviato-Troitskaia Lavra, 2009, p. 77.

for the new authorities, and was renamed Svomas,[32] Free State Art Studios. It consisted of an amalgam of a variety of workshops headed by different teachers. Sergei and Benatov chose the studio of Konchalovsky, who had been one of their teachers in the school of Mashkov.

KONCHALOVSKY, ART TRAINING

Konchalovsky was like a father figure to his students, caring for them and for their welfare. In his classes they received a solid basic art training in drawing, painting, composition and the appreciation of the Old Masters and their techniques. This was of great benefit to Sergei, who learned to appreciate and value these works. Even into old age he held a deep reverence for Rembrandt and among others, the compositional mastery of Veronese and the portraits of Tintoretto. Konchalovsky also imbued his students with his own admiration and love for Cézanne, who was widely recognized and appreciated in Russia at the start of the century.

For Sergei, Cézanne offered a further view into the expression of the eternal, he saw his work as having more of a spiritual quality than other contemporary painters. Cézanne, who is considered to be 'the father of modern painting', of cubism in particular, invented a system of dividing nature and any object into small components. His paintings as such are figurative, but on closer examination one can observe that the whole is fragmented into small 'cubes' of brush marks and other shapes; thus his paintings can be considered to be on the first step of abstraction.

Kandinsky considered that Cézanne's way of working was very close to a purely painterly method: "He raised the *nature morte* to a level where his objects animate what is inwardly *morte*. Cézanne treated these objects as he would a human being because he possessed the gift of seeing the inner life of all things."[33]

---

32. **Svo**bodnye gosudarstvennye khudozhestvennye **mas**terskie.
33. *The Life of Vasilii Kandinsky*, p. 70.

However, Konchalovsky disagreed with Cézanne's obsession for setting up perfect still-lifes, suggesting to his students that they rather observe alive and unspoilt nature. He would instruct the young artists to train their eye to pick out only the essential at first glance, finding a rhythm with mathematical forms in the 'melody' of the landscape and preferring the accurate proportions of the scene. This was naturally combined with studying the technique of colour application, rendering of shape and modeling shades and hues.

It is from Konchalovsky that Sergei got his solid professional training and understanding of art:

> Painting, like all other art, can only be great when it 'seizes' the whole man. If only a part of life is given over to it, it is amateurish. Amateur art never reaches the levels you can reach when your art is, in every respect, your life.[34]

It was through the effort of Konchalovsky that Sergei was finally released from his military service. Konchalovsky had written a letter of petition in February 1919,[35] asking for his gifted student to be freed from the army, as a prolonged absence was disruptive to his studies. Sergei, who was deeply affected by the atrocities surrounding him was profoundly grateful to his teacher for facilitating his release.

When Konchalovsky closed his workshop at the Svomas for the summer in 1920, he travelled as usual to Abramtsevo,the idyllic estate and artists' colony some 80 km north of Moscow. [36] Konchalovsky was accustomed to spending his summers there, painting and resting from the busy life of Moscow. He was especially drawn to the oak

---

34. *Letters to his Family*, p. 30.
35. RGALI, fond 680, op. 1, ed. khr. 967 (manuscript).
36. Abramtsevo had once been an artists' colony owned by Mamontov, the railway tycoon and art patron. Here all the great artists of the first Wanderers group would spend their summers, drawing, painting and creating. After Mamontov sold the property, it still held its attraction for artists due to its idyllic landscape and tranquility.

groves which he would paint repeatedly and often talk about to his students. He strove to depict the trees in such a way that the spectator could sense their deep roots. He would tell his students that to achieve a convincing painting of a tree it had to be constructed logically, like a building, starting from the ground and rising to the uppermost foliage. He would encourage his students to paint from nature, but having captured the initial inspiration and mapped out the colours and structures, it was then necessary for a serious study of plein-air to be worked out in the studio afterwards.

The image of the tree can be seen and interpreted in several ways. In the case of Konchalovsky, it is a purely painterly concern – to render the pictorial value of the tree, solid and monumental. The same image can however contain allegorical, historical and spiritual aspects.[37]

Sergei, in his later writings, reflects the same thought:

> When we see a centuries-old tree with its branches reaching to the clouds, we know that its roots, deep in the earth, must be powerful enough to support the whole. If the roots did not go down into the bowels of the earth – perhaps as far down as the tree is high – and if they were not as strong and widespread as the part we see, they could not feed the tree. They could not support it – a slight wind and the tree would fall.[38]

BARVIKHA

Inspired by their teacher Konchalovsky's example, in June 1920, when classes paused for the summer, Sergei, with a group of friends from the workshop, fled the turmoil of Moscow[39] to the rural idyllic

37. Cf. L. Tolstoy, *War and Peace*, book 2, part 3.
38. *His Life is Mine*, pp. 85-86.
39. Moscow had just experienced one of the worst winters, "Moscow in the early 1920's was a strange city… On the snowy streets lay fallen horses, in the evening shots rang out, fuel and foodstuffs were in very short supply." L. Senelick, S. Ostrovsky, *The Soviet Theater: A Documentary History,* New Haven: Yale University Press, 2014, p. 104.

countryside of the village of Barvikha, some 15 km west of Moscow. Barvikha was still a rural paradise with large trees, woods, meadows and lakes on the south bank of the river Moskva, far enough to be away from Moscow, but still fully accessible.[40] Here, they delighted in the calm and peaceful scenery, which provided the perfect setting for landscape painting, finding subjects to renew their inspiration and to restore their belief in life after the terrors of the recent years in the city.

It was a Russian equivalent of Barbizon,[41] the French village that had inspired a group of French painters in the mid 1800's to seek subjects for their painting, also at a time of political unrest and revolution.[42]

> A thousand such quiet little villages exist throughout the domains of the Gallic Republic, but none possesses such great attraction for the painter of the woodland, the plains, the quiet glades and pastures; for here nature seems to have spent herself in supplying material for pictorial representation.[43]

André Derain described the place:

> There was nothing yet there was everything, as in a truly great painting,' he added. Perhaps that is the real lesson of Barbizon.[44]

---

40. In the early 1900s the rail line had not yet been constructed as far as Barvikha; therefore the friends got off at the station of Nemchinovku and completed the journey on foot.
41. Like the French Barbizon, Barvikha got spoiled soon after this period; this time not by commercializing the artistic part, but by exploiting the fresh and healthy countryside with all its positive aspects. Lenin decided that a local sanatorium should be constructed, so as not to waste money on sending people abroad for healing. In 1935 the Barvikha sanatorium was established where all the major politicians, leaders, several writers and artists went for treatment. This brought with it a further development of luxury dachas and villas, which in their turn encouraged the building of nightclubs etc. Consequently present Barvikha has nothing in common with the Barvikha of some 100 inhabitants to which the young group of painters travelled in 1920 returning to nature, to find new, fresh and healthy inspiration.
42. The Barbizon painters partly reacted against the horrors of the 1848 revolutions, the first democratic uprisings and forerunners of the Russian revolutions.
43. A. Hoeber, *The Barbizon Painters Being the Story of the Men of Thirty*, New York: Frederick A. Stokes Company, 1915, p. 3.
44. J. Bouret, *The Barbizon School and 19th Century French Landscape Painting*, London: Thames and Hudson, 1973. p. 243.

Barvikha.

Photographs by Sergei Klishin, Cultural Centre "Barvikha".

A. Lebedev-Shuiskiy, *Siver willow*, 1921.
(https://artchive.ru/artists/23267~Anatolij_Adrianovich_LebedevShujskij)

The seven friends, in their early 20's, who went to Barvikha were:
Elena Fedorovna Anasova (1901-?)
Zoia Nikolaevna Bogoiavlenskaia (1899-?)
Leonardo Benatov (Leon Mikhailovich Bounatian) (1899-1972)
Anatolii Adrianovich Lebedev-Shuisky (1896 or 8?-1978)
Sergei Semeonovich Sakharov (1896-1993)
Grigori Alekandrovich Sretenskiy (1899-1972)
Aleksander Alekseevich Taldykin (1896-?) [45]

Of these, Lebedev-Shuisky and Sretenskiy later became well established artists in Russia. Tadiykin turned to theatre and scenic decorations, but the two female artists, Anasova and Bogoiavlenskaia disappeared from public view after 1920. Sergei and Benatov emigrated to France in 1922, where Benatov made a name for himself in the Parisian art world.

Grigori Sretenskiy had become a good friend of both Sergei and especially Benatov, with whom he kept a correspondence until the latter's death.[46]

The trip proved to be a turning point for the group, having a big influence on all of them. The young artists were captivated by the landscape which inspired their artistic expression. They "ecstatically painted studies of nature, giving especial attention to the representation and structure of trees: silver white willows, poplars, majestic oak trees and the spreading, branchy maple trees. To be immersed in the poetry of nature deeply affected the young artists' ability to see, feel and understand its beauty and developed an intensified feeling of colouring and poetic perception."[47] In Sergei's words: "The whole world, practically every visual scene, became mysterious, uncommonly beautiful, profound.

45. For short descriptions of their lives, see Appendix A.
46. The correspondence is kept at the Tretyakov gallery archives, fond 231, unpublished.
47. V. M. Lobanov, *Lebedev-Shuisky*, Moscow: Sovetskii khudozhnik, 1960, p. 10

Light changed, to caress and surround objects with a halo, as it were, of glory, imparting to them vibrations of life impossible for the artist to depict with the means at his disposal."[48] Throughout this time his search for a further, deeper truth was an underlying strong current: "When I was a painter I did not achieve satisfaction because the means at my disposal were impotent to portray the beauty of creation." [49]

Théodore Rousseau (1812-1867), one of the Barbizon painters, had felt the same, some 60 years earlier:

> I also used to hear the voices of the trees; their sudden, surprising movements, their variety of form and even the strange way in which they seemed to be attracted towards the light suddenly revealed to me the language of the forests. The whole vegetable world lived like a race of the dumb whose signs I guessed and whose passions I discovered. I wished to converse with them and to be able to tell myself, by means of this other language, painting, that I had laid my finger on the secret of their grandeur…You do not copy what you see with mathematical precision, but you feel and translate a real world in all of whose fatalities you are involved.[50]

On returning to Moscow, in the autumn of 1920, the influence of the expedition continued to have a lasting effect. The group members studied the examples of the Barbizon painters that were to be found in the Moscow museums and collections. They tried to understand how the Barbizon painters constructed and composed their paintings, which methods they used and how they arrived at their unique representation of nature. One of the members, Lebedev-Shuisky, described how he spent the autumn months attempting to grasp and develop the sharpness and intensely lyrical finesse which

48. *Wisdom*, p. 14.
49. *We Shall See Him*, p. 201.
50. A. Sensier, *Souvenirs sur Théodore Rousseau*, 1872, pp. 52, 111. Quoted in C. M. Kauffmann, *The Barbizon School*. London: Victoria and Albert Museum, 1965.

later characterized his work. "I have always been much drawn to willows of all colours and shades, I especially loved painting the grey willows on a grey day."[51] He also tried to divide the independence and originality of the creative expression from the artistic expression of nature. These observations and aspirations were shared by all the members of the group, not least Sergei.

The question of light became one of their main objects of study. As colour is only given full expression in relation to light, the value and amount of light depicted took on significant importance. Sergei paid special attention to this, concluding that light has to be rendered by using as little white paint as possible. It should be expressed by using colours transparently avoiding the use of white paint. In contrast, to express darkness, opacity of paint was the best method.

Sergei would use this inspiration later in life, when designing the gardens of his monastery, arranging the layout using principles of composition. He planted special trees that would cast shadows, giving them enough space to develop to their full glory. Other trees would be tied in order to help them grow straight, while some others would be cut to allow the more majestic ones to develop fully. It was architecture of space created with the eye of a painter. He also affirmed the teachings of Konchalovsky when instructing a young painter that, "*One cannot finish a work in plein-air, it has to be worked up into a tableau in the studio.*"[52]

'BYTIE' – MEANING OF 'BEING'

During all this time the question of eternity, of how to express the unattainable, of the search for *being*, had not abated but was continuing to gnaw away at both Sergei and Benatov. They found a certain solace in the summer spent in Barvikha, being able to express nature

51. Cf. Lobanov, *Lebedev-Shuisky,* p. 10.
52. All sentences in italics are from personal notes and sayings of Fr. Sophrony.

Some of the members of the 'Bytie' group. From left to right: P. Sokolov-Skalia, unknown, Z. Bogoiavlenskaia, P. Pokarzhevskii, L. Bounatian (Benatov), A. Lebedev-Shuiskiy, G. Sretenskiy.

(Otdel roukopisei Tretyakovskoi galerei, fond P. P. Sokolova-Skalia: fond 56, ed. khr. 24)

through the semi-abstract manner of Cézanne and thus touching on something further, something beyond. The other young painters of the group shared their quest; all felt an urge to escape from the current nightmarish situation, aspiring to a higher, more positive ideal. Their common aim was to try to find an expression for the eternal. It was in this context that Benatov came up with the idea that they should form an association to consolidate and further develop their ideas, and name it 'Bytie' (being). All agreed enthusiastically with the idea, both for the formation of the group and the descriptive name of their aim. They included two of their former classmates from the Mashkov school, who at the time were still studying with Mashkov, now at the Svomas: Pavel Petrovich Sokolov-Skalia (1899-1961) and Nikolai Pavlovich Razhin (1892-1942).[53]

At the beginning, the inspiration of the group was based on their spiritual quest, their aim to portray the eternal. All members were of the same heart and mind and put their entire efforts into their common goal through their painting. In the early years after the Revolution there was still a certain freedom, a euphoria where everybody sought to express what they thought about art and how they saw its future development. In later years this freedom was snuffed out and it was no longer possible to be open about one's inner strivings; thus with time, the group 'Bytie' moved in a new direction, promoting figurative art, and ultimately even adding socialist slogans to their exhibitions.

The young painters aimed to return to a more positive aspect of painting, to restore the mastery of the art of painting and to draw inspiration from nature.[54]

---

53. For a short description of their lives, see Appendix A.
54. The term 'positive' needs to be seen in relation to the general trend and state of painting, of art and of life in general. The early 1920's in Moscow was a time of extreme hardship and deprivation. This was naturally reflected in the arts, which were turning to the more materialistic trends of constructivism, moving towards industrialism.

The idea for the name, 'Bytie', came not only from their search for the eternal, but also from a painting class, when Konchalovsky was looking at the works of his students. Coming up to the easel of one of the pupils, he commented that the painting lacked substance and subject. He suggested: "Put some *being* into it". This phrase expressed exactly what the young painters wished to portray, an art with essence and content, *being* devoid of abstract and constructive designs. Yet, it did not aim at opposing the other visual arts, but was rather moving in a direction towards figurative art. As they belonged to the Russian school of Cézanne, which they had inherited from their teacher and the Knave of Diamonds group,[55] they were not painting nature in its pure realistic form, but in a form that was constructive in its own way. A contemporary artist comments: "Their aim was to portray content rather than form, yet at the same time the artists of 'Bytie' regarded the school of realism as negative. As followers of Cézanne they regarded the still-life as an object, indifferent to whether it was an apple, a worker or 'any object catching the eye'."[56] The realistic school was therefore considered negative insofar as it portrayed the object or person externally, bereft of inner life.

The Barbizon painters had answered to the new values and shapes of society by their 'revolution' of returning to nature for their source.

> The new theory – painting after nature, using fresh tones, and a careful relationship between light and colour rendered through short brushstrokes of sharp colours, bright reds, vivid indigo-blues, strong greens – was illustrated by a pragmatic painter rather than a theoretician.[57]

---

55. The 'Knave of Diamonds' group was formed in 1910 and exhibited until 1917, but the title continued in use to describe painters who painted in the 'Russian Cézannesque' style.
56. P. I. Lebedev, *Bor'ba za realizm v izobrazitel'nom iskusstve 20kh godov*, (The Fight for Realism in Fine Arts in the 20's) Moscow: Sovetskii khudozhnik, 1962, p. 12.
57. A. Parinaud, *Barbizon, the Origins of Impressionism*, Liechtenstien: Bonfini, 1994, p. 60.

In the same way, the young 'Bytie' painters responded to the social and visual situation of their time by expressing themselves through representations of nature. Their work was colourful and textured, though they did not confine themselves just to pictorial views of nature, but also painted still-lifes and some portraits.

The very fact that the 'Bytie' group advocated figurative painting, aiming through a positive statement to offer a solution to the turbulent times, was a revolutionary act in itself.

Their intentions were never meant as an opposition to the other art groups. This is clearly expressed in a letter from Benatov to Stretenskiy half a century later where he describes a visit of Camilla Gray[58] who had come to see him in Paris. She was searching for material for her book "The Russian Experiment in Art", looking for works by the constructivists, Tatlin, Malevich and Kandinsky. She was not interested in figurative art and had insisted that 'Bytie's' position was a protest against the wanderers, constructivists and suprematists. Benatov disagreed with her and as one of the founders, tried to explain his view but failed to convince her. However this disagreement was fortunate in that he later wrote a letter which clarified the true aim of the society.[59]

Benatov also wrote several other letters to Stretenskiy, complaining that later publications[60] about the society did not mention either his or Sergei's name. This omission is not surprising, since, as emigrants it was better their existence was not mentioned during the years of oppression. In his letters, Benatov who had been the first chairman, stated that the idea of the society sprung from visits to the collections

---

58. Camilla Gray (1936-1971) art historian, author of *The Great Experiment in Russian Art 1863-1922* (London: Thames and Hudson, 1986). It was printed in 1962 and was the first comprehensive study of modern Russian art.
59. Cf. Tretyakov archive, fond 231, ed. khr. 19 on 6 sheets, without date.
60. The publications Benatov mentioned were: V.M. Lobanov, *Khudozhestvennye gruppirovki za poslednie 25 let,* (The artistic groups of the last 25 years) Москва: 1930. Fedor Bogorodskii, *Moi tvorcheskii put'* (My creative path) Moskva, 1931.

of Shchukin and Morozov where all the latest French avant-garde was on show, although it was Cézanne who was the main inspiration.

In later publications, however, others claimed to have made significant contributions in setting up the society. After 1922, when Benatov and Sergei left the country, Lebedev-Shuisky was the chairman and later Konchalovsky in an honorary capacity, but in reality it seems that Stretenskiy was the driving force throughout.

The 'Bytie' group was welcomed and encouraged by a contemporary writer:[61] "The members of this artistic organization expressed their creative acts in beautiful and colourful searching, striving through painterly skill and mastery to portray the surrounding nature through the eyes of a new person."[62]

The use of the phrase 'New person' reflects on 'Bytie' in a more profound way, addressing the existential aspect of the name. Another writer of the time did not believe that the young VKhUTEMAS[63] students could have chosen a name with such a deep philosophical meaning on their own, but attributed it to their teacher, Konchalovsky.[64]

Sokolov-Skalia, one of the members of 'Bytie', summing up the situation of the young art students felt that they had to try to find their bearings. Most were concerned to serve the new state with their art in some way or other. This impetus gave wide scope for creativity and the development of ideas and so it was with enthusiastic anticipation that the young artists approached the promise of the new utopian state. Some specialised in large genre paintings, with their own

61. V.M. Lobanov (1885-1970), art historian.
62. Lobanov, *Lebedev-Shuisky*, p. 11.
63. In 1920 the Svomas were changed into a more organized structure, VKhUTEMAS: **V**ysshie gosudarstvennye **khu**dozhestvenno-**te**khnicheskie **mas**terskie, (Higher State Artistic-technical Workshops).
64. V. S. Turchin, *Obrazy bytia, ili iskusstvo sozertsaniia*, Moscow: Libri di Arte, 2008. p. 49.

strict rules of structure, colouring, depth, light and texture. Others, who considered that it was not the time to occupy themselves with the renewal of easel painting, turned towards monumental wall paintings, which was encouraged by the socialist leaders. Yet others devoted themselves to the art of the poster, in some cases approaching primitivism while in other cases employing abstract designs. All had their place but differed widely in expression. Everyone had received varied inspiration from some source or teacher and there was a common striving towards the future.[65]

Sergei shared the same zeal: "I was in a hurry to live. I did not want to waste a single hour, anxious to acquire as much knowledge as possible, not just in my own sphere of painting. I worked hard in my studio, which was spacious and quiet."[66]

During the most disturbed and difficult time of social unrest and the shortage of all essential provisions, Sergei still pursued his existential searching. The terrible conditions only intensified his urge to find a solution. His studio was in the same place as another of the 'Bytie' members, Sretenskiy which was at a considerable distance from both his house and the school. However, he considered that it was worth the hardship of getting there to enjoy the calm and peace that facilitated his work.

Apart from what was happening to the group and society at large, Sergei continued his own private quest for the meaning of life and the expression of eternity in painting:

> I had a studio in Borby Square, and as I worked there at my painting I was constantly preoccupied by the thought of transition to the *eternal.* I didn't like to put my mind to decorative art – we used to call it 'easel-art', meaning it was merely commercial.

---

65. Cf. Sokolov-Skalia in Turchin, *Obrazy bytia*, p. 48.
66. *We Shall See Him,* p. 15.

> My work on every landscape or portrait took hours and hours. And my thinking would be lost in the feeling of the mystery of nature. Usually we encounter the phenomenon that people look at objects – the sky, a house, a tree, people – simply to find their orientation. But for me each one of these was an inexpressible mystery. It was a wonder to me – how this vision comes into being. From such a way of looking at things the sense of beauty develops, because the deeper you penetrate the extraordinary complexity of every phenomenon in life, the more you are aware of its beauty. Under this influence the feeling of beauty sometimes used to grow in me to such an extent that I completely lost awareness of time. Of course, it's difficult to recount those long days I spent in the studio – sometimes from morning until late at night.[67]

In addition to this example of losing the consciousness of time from the impact on him of beauty, he also describes another similar occasion when painting his sister[68] and pondering on one of his questions about eternal life.

> Once I was painting Maria's portrait, and the thought came to me: 'How can we cross beyond the boundary of death?' Three hours went by, and, honestly, I did not feel that time passing at all; for me it could have been ten minutes. And then I noticed tears running down Maria's face. I said, 'Maria, what is it?' 'I can't take any more. I'm tired.' We looked at the clock: I had been painting her for three hours without a break. This was one episode which Maria witnessed. And such episodes occurred very often.[69]

As mentioned in the passage above, Sergei and his friends did not agree with easel painting. One could argue that their plein-air paintings

---

67. *Letters to his Family*, p. 25.
68. His sister, Maria Kalashnikova, née Sakharova, (1903- 1986), was in 1922 also enrolled as a student at VKhUTEMAS, in the industrial and production department.
69. *Letters to his Family,* p. 28.

were easel paintings, since they were done on either canvas or boards, but in their view they were different. 'Easel-art' was considered to be decorative art.[70] As such, it stood for bourgeois art, strictly realistic and fully figurative, reflecting the academic style mentioned above. That their own plein-air painting happened to be painted on canvas or board which in order to be worked, needed the support of an easel, did not mean it was 'easel art'. They were equally opposed to the strictly realistic work of the Wanderers, criticizing them for having let their ideas prevail and neglecting the artistic side of painting. What the 'Bytie' group was aiming for was a positive, transformed and transfigured view of nature and still-lifes, devoid of the superfluous detail and decoration, that were to be found in palaces. Their ideal was the beauty of the real world, the world that still existed in spite of the turbulent and difficult times. They were influenced in this respect by their teacher, Konchalovsky, who in all vicissitudes managed to see the best and uplifting side of life and only painted that.[71] It was not a case of escaping the suffering, but of rising above it, focusing on higher levels than the unbearable day to day attempt at survival.

The group also had their own attitude towards academic teaching. They were firmly convinced that the academy was unable to produce any artists; at best, the graduates could become art historians or art critics. They felt that the rigid teaching discipline of the academy stifled any inspiration and talent in its students. Creativity and innovation were something foreign to the Academy for the teaching was still modeled

70. Kandinsky also had a dislike for decorative art, cf. Kandinsky's vision, *The Life of Vasilii Kandinsky*, p. 48. "It is not obvious (geometrical) constructions that will be richest in possibilities for expression, but hidden ones, emerging unnoticed from the canvas and meant less for the eye than for the soul." *Ibid.* p. 49.
71. Konchalovsky's wife Olga recalls how after the Revolution, they had lived in hardship using only one room because of the lack of fuel and yet they had felt a new liberation, as from slavery. They could not understand some other painters who had left the country now that there was more freedom. "We loved the West very much but it did not even occur to us to leave our Motherland when it had just discovered life, free of the rich art collectors' dictate." (*The Unknown Konchalovsky*, Chronicle, 1918, Notes by O.V. Konchalovsky.)

on the nineteenth century neoclassical academies of Western Europe. "The academic system of art education relied substantially on life drawing and on copying from 'originals', that is, from professors' drawings and from plaster casts of antiquities. Life drawing formed the basis of the general academic program, and its exclusive position accounts for the high level of draftsmanship among its students."[72] After such a restricted training it was obvious to the 'Bytie' friends that a graduate was quite incapable of true and free creation. The same thought is expressed by the artist Pavel Filonov (1883-1941), who had himself suffered from his passage through the academy: "...[within] the present state of the Academy pedagogical program, ... the pupil is kept obedient to the program and his professors out of fear of being expelled. As a result, the human being in him is forgotten and a slave, a lackey to the Academy structure is made out of him."[73]

THE FIRST EXHIBITION

In December 1921 the group arranged their first exhibition. They borrowed rooms from the Shor Brothers' music school at the 'Myasnitskaya Gates', where Mashkov also had his studio. It was one block away from their own school VKhUTEMAS and since the workshops of Konchalovsky and Mashkov were affiliated it was the obvious place for the first exhibition of 'Bytie'.

The exhibition opened on the 1st January 1922.

We have no information as to what kind of works Sergei exhibited; all we know is that he was one of the participants. Judging from the reviews of the critics, the works on show were all bright, colourful landscapes and still-lifes. As such they were in strong contrast to their period, both in ethos and style.

---

72. Nicoletta Misler, "Sergei Konenkov and His Connection to Western Art", *The Uncommon Vision of Sergei Konenkov*, New Brunswick: Rutgers University Press, 2001, p. 138.
73. P. Filonov, "Lecture at a Conference in the Department of Painting at the Academy of Arts", N. Misler and J. E. Bowlt, *Pavel Filonov: A Hero and His Fate*, Austin, Texas: Silvergirl, Inc., 1983, p. 203.

One of the visitors recalls:

> It was cold, the visitors walked through the rooms in fur coats with turned up collars. On the walls hung paintings, mainly landscapes and still-lifes, which impressed me with their materiality and their freshness. Next to one painting that was somehow very brightly coloured stood a tall youth with long black hair. Gesticulating with widespread arms he argued with an interlocutor from the public:
>
> 'You understand, we are fed up with abstraction! Life should resound in our canvases! Do you understand! Life!' This was the young painter Sokolov-Skalia.[74]

Another visitor describes their impression of the scene:

> In the very first days of January 1922 the first exhibition of 'Bytie' opened. It was huddled in a small room of the music studio of the brothers Shor on Myasnitskaya.
>
> The canvases, drawings and sculptures of the seven founding members were exhibited in a tiny room. The young artists were eager to hear the opinion of the older painters.
>
> The most energetic of the group was the thin and tall Pavel Sokolov-Skalia who, dressed in a long grey English coat, approached the visitors, asking them about their impressions of the exhibition. He was the spokesman of the group, while the others timidly answered questions and gave explanations.
>
> After all it was not a small thing that the opening of the 'Bytie' exhibition was straight after the exhibitions of 'The Union of Artists' and especially of 'The World of Art', whose president, Il'ia Mashkov, was their teacher. He himself was present at

74. F. Bogorodskiy about the first exhibition of 'Being', Turchin, *Obrazy bytia*, p. 47.

Sergei Sakharov, *Still-life*, 1922. Private collection.

> the opening, enthusiastically and cheerfully encouraging his disciples. He did not hide the faults of his students, but neither underestimated their successes. …
>
> The exhibition attracted much attention and was widely discussed. The press was very sympathetic to the initiatives of the young artists. …
>
> The artists of ‘Bytie’ concerned themselves about the problem of new content and of the picture with complete form.[75]

There was no exhibition catalogue and the only material available is from the recollections of visitors who wrote about it. At this time, ‘Bytie’ did not have any slogans or special ideologies. Their aim, to express eternity, was kept secret. Idealistic statements about their work came later. From the 3rd exhibition in 1925 until the 7th and final exhibition in 1929 there were catalogues and with them various socialist statements taking a firm stance against constructivism and all non-figurative art, but as mentioned above, the first exhibition was not meant as a protest or an attack on anyone.

The critics were favorable:

> With all their hot youthfulness asserted in dispute and discussion of the principles of ‘Russian Cézannism’, they in their very creativity went away from the lessons of Cézanne, even further than their teachers, closer to the painting of etudes placing themselves in the middle between plein-air works following the ‘Society of Russian Artists’ and the light-transparent cloths of the French impressionists.[76]

They observed that the students had absorbed everything that their masters, Konchalovsky and Mashkov, had to offer them as well as

75. Lev Varshavskii, in Lebedev, Bor’ba, p. 115.
76. Turchin, *Obrazy bytia,* p. 135.

working in the style of Cézanne, but that theirs was not a pointless art. They congratulated the young artists on having passed through the VKhUTEMAS without being touched by the unfavorable conditions there (probably referring to the adversities and quarrels). They felt that in spite of all the difficulties the students faced and by overcoming them, their art was progressive.

Of the pictures exhibited, Sokolov-Skalia, who had presented 9 works, was singled out as having a strong drawing technique and the potential of becoming a future master. His works were in the japono-impressionistic style. All others were considered gifted, and were praised for their richly coloured landscapes and still-lifes. There was also a sculpture by Bourov[77] in the exhibition, called 'The Model', which was considered masterly. "On the whole, the youngsters, debuting at this exhibition, deserve attention and encouragement."[78]

The art critic who understood them best was A.A. Sidorov (1891-1978), who, though mainly interested in graphic art and the art of the book, still appreciated novelty and innovation, which found expression in his interest in modern art. He wrote about contemporary art and he had the following to say regarding the exhibition:

> In the history of contemporary art, surely the new young artists are of the most interest, exemplified in the exhibition of the group 'Bytie', who at this time occupied a very curious place in between the right wing 'Society' and the left wing 'World of Art'.
>
> For the historian it is very noticeable that this youth did not lean towards either of these factions. The students of P.P.Konchalovksy and I.I.Mashkov found in themselves the boldness to stand independently on their own two feet. The

77. Apart form the members of 'Bytie', two architects had been invited to participate in the exhibition. *Cf.* Turchin, *Obrazy bytia*, p. 153.
78. D. Melnikov, "The exhibition of paintings of 'Being'." Turchin, *Obrazy bytia*, pp. 79-80.

level of their mastership is doubtlessly high. We will leave for the future the critical evaluation of their caliber and gift.

What we affirm to be important for history is the fact that in our days there exists a group of young painters who are brave enough to go against the current tide of classical form in part typified by Rembrandt, Michelangelo and Ingres. It raises the question would the old form continue to direct western art?

The example of the exhibition of 'Bytie' suggests not.[79]

Sidorov states clearly the unique and non-conformist position of the group, that they were siding neither with the right-, nor with the left–wing artists, but rather expressed their convictions, standing 'on their own feet', which in the prevailing movement of art at that time was both a courageous and brave act of faith.

Sergei and Benatov left Russia 7 months after this event. Benatov still presented some work in the second exhibition the following year. Sergei received a letter from Sretenskiy describing this second exhibition as having been a success "in the ideological sense".[80] The work of Sretenskiy, and later of his wife Nina Stenshinskaya (1901-1988) who also joined the 'Bytie' society, continued in a progressive, slightly stylized figurative 'Russian Cézannesque' style throughout their lives.

MOVING ON

Sergei had long been looking for a way to leave Russia, fearing to be drawn into the red army again and knowing that he could be imprisoned a third time which would likely end in execution. The

79. A. A. Sidorov, *Sredi kollektsionerov*, 1922, N° 2 (February) in Turchin, *Obrazy bytia*, p. 81. ("Observations of the history of contemporary artistic life" in the February issue of *Among Collectors.*) It is unclear whether the two sculptors Adrianova and Bourova were additional non-recorded members, or if they only participated in the exhibition.
80. Quote from Sretenskiy's own words. This letter does not exist anymore. The information comes from a letter from Sergei to E. Lourié in February 1923.

uncertainty of the times was unbearable, arrests were common and many people disappeared without a trace. It was a tradition for Russian artists to visit Italy and Paris at some time in the beginning of their career and when Benatov received a grant to study abroad, Sergei decided to join his friend. They travelled south on a long and perilous train journeythrough the areas where just a few months previously the civil war had raged, to visit Benatov's family who were staying at the Black Sea. In August 1922, they sailed from Novorossiysk on a Turkish ship, heading straight for Italy. Upon their arrival in Italy, which at the time was strongly opposed to communism, they were stopped and suspected of being Russian spies. To prove that they were painters, they produced some drawings, which were taken to a local dignitary and art collector. He was so pleased with their work that he gave them hospitality in his castle.[81] After visiting the artistic sites of Italy, they travelled on to Berlin where they spent the autumn, painting and visiting galleries. Here they met up with their former classmate from Konchalovsky's studio, Eugenia Lourié, who had recently married Boris Pasternak. During that autumn Berlin hosted the First All Russian Art exhibition, where they saw the work of their compatriots and contemporaries. In late 1922 they travelled on to Paris, where they both settled. For Sergei the question of a return to Russia remained open for many years, being torn between the pain of separation from his own home, the hardships of emigration and the uncertainty of what would be awaiting him upon his return.

81. It is highly possible that the dignitary in question was Gabriele D'Annunzio, since all the external descriptions fit his image. It has however, to date, not been possible to find any evidence.

CHAPTER 2

Being, non-being and the Abyss

> IN PETERSBURG THE PAVEMENTS are out of glass. Underneath there is a void ... the modernists are used to walk above the abyss. … The abyss is a must for the Petersburg writer. … They go and fall in love above the abyss, they visit each other above the abyss, make their careers above the abyss, and place the samovar above the abyss.
>
> Oh, this beloved abyss![82]

This was the state of the Russian artists and writers in the first decade of the 20th century. Sergei was very much part of this, as he himself expresses,

> I can remember myself as I was then, behaving in everyday life like any of my contemporaries though there were moments when I could not feel the earth under my feet. I could see it with my eyes in the ordinary way but in spirit I was moving over a bottomless abyss.[83]

In the early 20th century, during the Apocalyptic time of the Russian Silver Age, the abyss was used as an image to describe the fleeting nature of the insecure and unstable world of that time. Set against this was the image of the homely samovar, demonstrating what an every day reality the prevailing sense of the abyss had become.

---

82. B. Bugaev (=A. Belyi): "Shtempelevannaia kalosha" in Vesy, 1907, no. 5, pp.49-50, partly quoted in: John E. Bowlt, *Moscow & Petersburg 1900-1920, Art, Life & Culture*, New York: Vendome Press, 2008, p. 319. We Shall See Him, p. 31.
83. *We Shall See Him*, p. 12.

Sergei Simeonovich Sakharov, 1918.
(RGALI, fond 680, op. 4, ed. khr 73. “Lichnoe delo Sakharova Sergeia Simenovicha”, 9 ioulia 1918, list 3)

Sergei Simeonovich Sakharov, *Self-portrait*,1918. Private collection.

Sergei's life coincided with a turbulent political time. In 1904, when he was 8 years old, war broke out with Japan, with its disastrous outcome the following year. Russia suffered heavy losses and the general morale of the country was deeply shaken. Social unrest had been simmering for several decades, resulting in the first revolution in 1905. Then followed several years of various failed attempts at democracy, culminating with the abdication of the Tsar in early 1917 and the coup d'état of the Bolsheviks later that year. In addition there was Russia's involvement in World War 1, from 1914 until a devastating defeat in 1918, when civil war broke out, which caused even more bloodshed and lasted until 1920 with sporadic fighting which continued in the provinces until 1923. At the same time the economy had collapsed, which combined with the drought and failed crops of 1920 and 1921, resulted in famine and a general state of disaster.

Sergei, growing up at this time was deeply affected by the events. In his own words,

> The atmosphere reeks with the smell of blood. Day after day the universe is fed with news of the slaying or torture of the vanquished in fratricidal conflicts. Black clouds of hate screen the heavenly Light from our eyes. People make their own hell for themselves.[84]

Street fighting was rife in Moscow and suffering everywhere prevalent. There was a constant fear of being arrested and shot. Nobody could escape the uncertainty of what would happen next. The meaninglessness of the whole situation tormented Sergei. As a result, his own spiritual and existential questions became increasingly his intense preoccupation.

84. *We Shall See Him*, p. 31.

> I did not understand why I was born. To give up my life in the whirlpool of historic events for the sake of an ideal that I had not yet consciously grasped? That is how the memory of death was born in me, together with an awareness of the absurdity of all earthly possessions. … My attention gradually turned from all my surroundings and concentrated within me, focusing on the question 'is man eternal, or are we all to return to the darkness of non-being?' My soul was pining in search for an answer to the question that had become more important for me than whatever was happening in the world. Everything was collapsing around me but I barely noticed what was going on. … I was young, eighteen years old, but even then I had the feeling that every man is himself, in a sense, the focal point of all the universe. [85]

Sergei immersed himself into his art tirelessly seeking to find a solution through his painting. The question of eternity had been the preoccupation of most artists; all striving to express the eternal, to grasp what is beyond time, to find a solution and a reason for life. This striving had always been particularly strong among the Russian artists, but it greatly intensified in the hardship and general suffering of the time. Sergei read, searched and studied all writers, painters and thinkers from the decades before him, who had tried to express their experiences of eternity.

Already in the 19th century, Vladimir Soloviev (1853-1900), a precursor of the Symbolists,[86] had sought to express the meaninglessness of conventional life:

---

85. A. Sophrony, *Tainstvo khristianskoi zhizni,* Sergiev Posad: Sviato-Troitskaia Lavra,, 2009, p. 77.

86. The Symbolist movement in Russia, which differs from European Symbolism in that it concentrates more on eternal and existential questions than its western counterparts, is usually dated 1885-1910, but earlier traces can be found already in the 19th century with the philosopher and poet Vladimir Soloviev (1853-1909).

Dear friend, do you not see
That everything we see is but
Reflections, shadows of that which is
Invisible to our sight? [87]

This was one of the inspirations of the Russian Symbolists. Their main aim was to break free from the earthly into a mystical and eternal sphere; as such they had a psychological, and to a certain extent spiritual, 'revolt' against all earlier social and moral values. The members of this movement felt that the old descriptive language, both in word and the visual 'language' of figurative art, could no longer express and convey unique personal emotions and feelings. They aimed for a mystical, transcendental expression, and, as such, were in search of eternity. In their quest they naturally came across eastern mysticism and the occult. The colour blue (or azure) was of special significance to them, "…it was reminiscent of a basic concept of symbolist philosophy: for the symbolists 'blue' was the description of the ulterior world, of the higher, spiritual reality and was a key word of their vocabulary." [88]

The Symbolist artists and philosophers interpreted the colour azure in a variety of ways at different levels. Blue also held certain mystical connotations which found expression in various forms.

Sergei shared their fascination with blue. "When I was young I liked to lie on the bench in the garden and look up at the blue sky. Later I understood that blue light is an image of transcendence. There is nothing similar on earth to the blue colour of the sky." [89]

---

87. Vladimir Soloviev, "Mily drug …", *Stikhotvoreniia* (Moscow, 1915), p. 111. Quoted in: D.S. von Mohrenschildt, *The Russian Symbolist Movement, PMLA,* Vol. 54, No. 4. (Dec 1938), p. 1193.
88. J. E. Bowlt, *Russian Art 1875-1975, A Collection of Essays,* New York: MSS Information Corporation, 1976, p. 76.
89. From a manuscript by Fr. Sophrony where he sketched down his thoughts for an introduction of *His Life is Mine,* unpublished archive, in Russian.

He would gaze into the depths of the blue sky until he damaged his eyes and had to be blindfolded for a number of days for his eyes to heal.

> I always considered that the wonderfully deep heavens that we could see were not a 'wall' around the earth; that beyond the limits of the visible lay reality that is boundless, cosmic, and inaccessible like the visible sky. Lying in the roof of my studio, I used to gaze attentively at the sky, and in a strange way it seemed to come nearer to me, so close that it seemed to encompass me too. But it did not communicate its *Mystery* to me. Oh, how I looked at every object, at every sight, with passion; and each phenomenon, each object, became mysterious. How is it possible that a ray of light, in itself something simple, divides into an infinite variety of hues, but acting as a whole it creates a picture which is forever alive, which changes unceasingly, and yet preserves something of oneness? [90]

In later life he developed a special shade of grey green blue, which gave a sense of space and infinity, using it as a colour for the ceilings in his chapels, to express the boundless expanse of the sky, and eternity.

Sergei followed the exploits of the Symbolists, reading them and attending their exhibitions, studying their thoughts, as he also searched for the eternal.

> In those years I read books about Buddhism, yoga, and other mystical books. And it seemed to me that the Gospel was less profound than the other teachings. The thought came to me that the Gospel said, 'Love God and your neighbour'. So I reflected: 'This is just psychology', whereas the other teachings spoke about a supra-personal Absolute. Insofar as I loved very much to pray, my prayer preserved my love for Christ, so that I did

---

90. *Letters to his Family*, p. 279.

not reject my past. But the new discovery seemed to me more profound. … two things dominated my thoughts at that time: one, the idea of the supra-personal Absolute, and the other, how man could get beyond the confines of this brief small life. By that I mean that man's spirit cannot accept the idea of death. As I recall, at that time the words of Pushkin had an enormous influence over me:

No, I'll not wholly die:
My soul in sacred lay
Shall outlive my dust
And escape decay. [91]

Pushkin,[92] who himself was also tormented with existential questions, frequently used metaphors of azure as well as of the abyss in his writings. According to a contemporary Russian writer, "in every word [of Pushkin] there is an abyss of space".[93]

Another writer who was influenced by the expressive language of Symbolist mysticism was Pavel Florensky (1882-1937).[94] He developed several views on the arts, notably on the synthetic vision of the artist in creating a timeless, whole portrait of a person, expressing this symbolically by describing it as a mystical tree of life.

Though it seems Sergei neither met nor studied with him, there is nonetheless a certain resemblance in their thought,[95] especially about

---

91. *Letters to his Family,* p. 28.
92. Alexander Pushkin (1977-1837), Russia's most famous poet playwright and novelist.
93. N. V. Gogol, *Polnoe sobranie sochinenii,* 14 vols., Moscow: Nauka, 1937-52, vol. viii, p. 55.
94. Pavel Florensky was not only a philosopher, but also a mathematician, engineer, inventor, art historian, theologian and, from 1911, an orthodox priest. He is often called "The Russian Leonardo Da Vinci". Florensky taught perspective and analysis of space at VKhUTEMAS from 1921 until 1924, but there is no evidence that Sergei attended these classes or was present at any of his lectures.
95. His views on Sophia were not shared by Fr. Sophrony.

their experience of light and darkness. Florensky, who was very much a representative of his time, describes a dream he once had:

> A darkness without a ray of light, almost palpably dense surrounded me. Some force was dragging me to the brink; I felt that this was the limit of God's being and that beyond it was absolute nothingness. I wanted to cry out and could not. I knew that in another moment I should be thrust into outer darkness. Darkness began to fill my whole being. I almost lost consciousness of myself and I knew that this was absolute metaphysical annihilation.[96]

The concept of outer darkness and of falling into a void of non-being bore relation to Sergei's own experience. The ever-present abyss and the constant reminder of death followed him everywhere. In his own words,

> Perpetual oblivion, as the extinguishing of the light of consciousness, filled me with horror. This state of spirit settled in me, against my will. Everything that was happening in the world reminded me forcibly of the inevitability of an end to human history. A vision of the abyss was always there, only occasionally allowing me a moment's peace.[97]

This vision of the abyss remained with Sergei throughout his life. With time as his life changed, it evolved into other dimensions with new meanings and images nonetheless awesome. It always stayed, holding out a promise, reminding him of hope and a vision of what lay beyond.

All contemporary artists responded to the extremities of the times by intensifying their attempts to deal with the instability of the situation. The violence, wars, sufferings and torments spurred their creativity as they tried to find expression for their feelings and offer solutions.

---

96. N. Lossky, *History of Russian Philosophy,* New York: International Universities Press, 1951, pp. 185-186.
97. *We Shall See Him,* p. 12.

Yet for Sergei the situation became increasingly meaningless and absurd.

> With the outbreak of the First World War the problem of eternity began to predominate in my mind. The news of thousands of innocent victims being killed at the front placed me squarely before a vision of tragic reality … if the will of evil powers could create such a state of affairs, where was the sense of our presence in this world? And I … why was *I* born? I had only just begun to perceive myself as a human being: my heart was aglow with good intentions, seeking perfection like all young people, aspiring to the light of universal knowledge.[98]

He immersed himself in his language of painting, hoping by transcending it to gain new horizons and find expression for the eternal and the answers to his questions.

> Art was for me a way to gain knowledge of being. That was how I perceived it, how I lived in it. It required the whole of me; even more than the whole. Unless one submits oneself to art entirely, it never becomes genuine, i.e. such an art that takes its servant beyond the limits of time and space. Truly artistic is only a work that carries inside elements of the eternal; else, it remains just an ornamental decoration of our dwelling.[99]

Other artists shared the same urge to express the eternal, how to break out of the temporal and through art, writing and other creative paths find a solution to all questions. Art seemed the path and way forward as they all focused on eternity.

> The beauty of the world around combined with the miracle of the dawning vision enthralled me. But in my art I tried to sense,

98. *We Shall See Him*, pp. 10-11.
99. A. Sophrony, *Rozhdenie v Tsarstvo nepokolbimoe,* Moscow: Palomnik, 2000, p. 163.

> beyond visible reality the invisible, timeless essence which afforded me moments of exquisite delight.[100]

The generation of painters before Sergei, some of whom later became his teachers, had turned to Cézanne's method as a solution to express the eternal. Cézanne had brought the conception of purely figurative art to another level – taking out the narrative aspect and placing his objects or scenery in a timeless frame – thus even to a certain extent giving a 'being' to his still-lifes.

Kandinsky valued Cézanne highly,

> He knew how to create a living being out of a teacup or, rather, how to recognize such a being within this cup. He can raise the 'still-life' to a level where externally 'dead' objects come alive internally. He treated these objects just as he does people, for he had the gift of seeing inner life everywhere. He expressed them in terms of color, thus creating *an inner, painterly note, a sound,* and molds them into a form that can be raised to the level of abstract sounding, harmonious, often mathematical formulae.[101]

For Sergei, however, it was Kandinsky himself who held the greater attraction, as he combined the spiritual with art and thus answered some of Sergei's deeper questions, which went beyond the realms of art itself.

> The spiritual life – one part which is art (among the prime movers of the spiritual life) – is a complex movement, but it is a distinct one and can be expressed in a simple formula: forwards and upwards. This movement is the path of cognition. It can assume various forms, but at its basis there always lies the same inner meaning, the same aim.[102]

---

100. *We Shall See Him,* p. 15.
101. *On the Spiritual in Art (1920),* Experiment Vol. 8, p. 81.
102. *Ibid,* p. 64.

Kandinsky had the vision that it was possible to relate to a work of art as having a life in its own right. He considered that true creation was only possible if the artist himself had an inner life with which he could transfuse his painting enabling it to take on its own eternal being. The picture then presents both an outer and inner life, the outer, being its visible form and the inner, the invisible and spiritual dimension. The artist had to put himself at the service of his art, allowing it space to have its own spiritual life and value rather than imposing himself upon it, forcing its direction. This in turn gives the spectator opportunity to engage in a relationship with the work to the extent that he becomes a co-creator. Thus the creative process continues in the form of a dialogue between the spectator and work of art even after its completion.

Sergei set out to follow Kandinsky's creative ideas, which were in the realm of 'pure painting', as Kandinsky himself called his abstract art. Sergei found this lent itself well to express his inner agonized state. Kandinsky, who also sought to express the impersonal absolute, thought art had prophetic possibilities in that,

> … cosmic tragedy in which the human element is only one sound, only a single voice, whose focus is transported to within a sphere that approaches the divine…I am speaking not about my own pictures, but about a kind of art that has never yet been personified and in its abstract being still waits for incarnation.[103]

Sergei began to explore these new ways which had opened for him, searching for pure expression and new creations. It did not however give him a direct answer to his questions about suffering and the meaning of life. Yet it brought him to unexpected new thresholds offering a direction in which lay the ultimate fulfillment of his quest.

103. *Complete Writings*, p. 398.

> (abstract art) engrossed me for two or three years and led to the first theological thought to originate within my own mind.... I soon realized that it was not given to me, a human being, to create from 'nothing', in the way that only God can create. I realized that everything that I created was conditional by what was already in existence. I could not invent a new colour or line that had never existed anywhere before. An abstract picture is like a string of words, beautiful and sonorous in themselves, perhaps, but never expressing a complete thought. In short, an abstract picture represented a disintegration of being, a falling into the void, a return to the *non esse* from which we had been called by the creative act of God. I therefore abandoned my fruitless efforts to devise something new, and the problem of creative work now became closely linked in my mind with the cognition of Being.[104]

Sergei, having abandoned the path of abstraction, sought next to express the eternal by reproducing the beauty of nature. His new aim was to reach the Creator through the creation. His idea was that by copying the work of the Creator he might draw nearer to Him whose existence he had begun to perceive. There were even moments when he thought that he had reached his goal,

> ...for a brief moment there comes a feeling of triumph, of victory. I have grasped what I was seeking! Surely I am close now to expressing the beauty spread before my eyes. But the rapture would soon disappear and once more I would be tormented by my failure.[105]

However art failed to offer respite from the oppressive thought that death pervaded everything and this continued to dominate and torment

104. *Wisdom*, pp. 13-14.
105. A. Sophrony, *On Prayer*, Tolleshunt Knights: Stavropegic Monastery of St John the Baptist, 1996, p. 51.

him. There were moments when he did not feel the earth beneath his feet, other moments when leaning his head on his hands, he had a sensation of holding a scull in his hands, yet he was still a young and healthy man. Slowly and gradually, over a long period of time, he turned back to the God of his childhood and once more started praying.

Life set over the abyss was an image for the Russian modernists to the extent that they even embraced the samovar in its context. Later in life, in a different context, when a hermit came and asked him about spiritual life, he advised: "Stay at the edge of the abyss, and when it gets too much, step back from the edge and take a cup of tea."[106]

106. *Letters to his Family,* p. 35.

Sergei Sakharov, *Dunes*, early 1920s. Painting destroyed in fire.

CHAPTER 3

From the abyss to the knowledge of *Being*

> SOMETIMES THE TRIALS AND difficulties which befall put us in the position of a traveller who suddenly finds himself on the edge of an abyss from which it is impossible to turn back. The abyss is the darkness of ignorance, and terror at being captive to death.[107]

Sergei's questions about death, mortality and eternity were considerably intensified by the acute suffering of the world in all the tragedy of war and revolution and the further catastrophe of civil war. It seemed to him that life was futile and senseless if it was to end in eternal *non-being*.

> Perpetual oblivion, as the extinguishing of the light of consciousness, filled me with horror.... A vision of the abyss was always there ... My ever-increasing consciousness of death attained such force that the world, this whole world of ours, seemed like a mirage liable at any moment to vanish into an everlasting void.[108]

His ever-present sense of death and eternal oblivion, became so acute that all the catastrophes and calamities around him paled in front of the interior horror he experienced. If everything was going to die and disappear into a void, what was the purpose of it all? This vision went so far that he saw everything and everybody in the shadow of death and destruction.

> In me, with me, all that had formed part of my consciousness would die: people close to me, their suffering and love, the whole historical progress, the universe in general, the sun, the

107. *His Life is Mine,* p. 61.
108. *We Shall See Him,* p. 12

> stars, endless space; even the Creator of the world Himself – He, too, would die in me. In short, all life would be engulfed in the darkness of oblivion.[109]

Paradoxically, Sergei did not despair, but felt that there had to be an answer to the suffering he experienced. This feeling made him start to look for the reason of existence, for the purpose of *being* and eternity. For a while he thought that he could find the answer to his quest in art. He worked long and hard at his painting, trying to express the eternal. In addition to this he turned to Eastern religions, thinking that eternity was to be attained in losing oneself in an absolute *being*. He continued down this path for some 4 or 5 years, feeling occasional relief from his acute suffering in the practice of meditation, but his inner search was not satisfied. He sensed that he was suspended above a bottomless abyss but at the same time had come up against a heavy impenetrable leaden wall.

> I never said a word to anyone about my 'parallel' life in the spirit – nothing prompted me to such self-revelation. What was taking place in me proceeded from some superior source, independent of my will or any initiative on my part. I did not understand what was happening in me and yet I held it sacred.[110]

Somehow, throughout this period, though he had consciously stopped himself praying, his heart was kept intact and within a glimmer of hope lived on. Through this small flame a tiny crack eventually appeared in the leaden wall which became pierced by a ray of light,

> … a new vision of the world and its meaning opened before me. Side by side with devastation I contemplated rebirth.[111]

---

109. *We Shall See Him*, p.12.
110. *We Shall See Him,* p. 15.
111. *His Life is Mine*, p. 38.

This small presence of light in his otherwise oppressive inner darkness, slowly and gently revealed the true nature of *being* to him. He was given to understand that the author of life is a person, a *Being*, knowable and attainable. With this discovery he started praying again, asking the *Being* to reveal himself. Slowly, through different experiences he came to the knowledge that Christ was this *Being,* the Creator and author of life.

> We would never be able to know the true God if He Himself did not bridge the chasm which lies between Him and us, created beings. Our God is not a human invention but the One Who truly IS, the true God, Who from His excessive love, reveals Himself to man.[112]

Sergei gave himself over to prayer, striving to come closer to *the Being,* his whole aim now was to learn to know and enter into a personal contact with *Him.*

> I was filled with reverent worship for the First Craftsman, the Creator of all things, and a longing to meet Him, learn from Him, know how He created.[113]

At the same time Sergei was filled with an ardent prayer of repentance for having turned his back on Christ in the search of, what he thought, was a more absolute union with eternity but which in fact lead him to that very eternal oblivion he was trying to escape. The prayer engulfed his entire being and came into conflict with his painting, which also demanded the whole of him. The struggle between these two forms of art – prayer being an even higher form of art than painting – tore him apart and he realized he would have to choose between them. For a while he tried to combine the two, but ultimately he realized that prayer was the more important for him and he gave up painting.

---

112. A. Zacharias, *Man the Target of God*, Tolleshunt Knights: Stavropegic Monastery of St. John the Baptist, 2015, p. 250. Archimandrite Zacharias was one of Father Sophrony's close disciples and has written much expounding and clarifying Father Sophrony's thoughts and theology.
113. *Wisdom*, p. 14.

> This battle between art and prayer, that is, between two forms of life which require the whole of man, continued within me in a very intense manner for a year and a half or two years. In the end I was convinced that the means at my disposal in art would not give me what I was looking for. That is, even if I could intuitively sense eternity through art, this awareness is not as deep as in prayer. And I decided to give up art – which for me was a terribly high price to pay.[114]

The gradual recognition of the nature of a personal *Being* Who was God and Creator took place in Paris over the period of time from 1923 to 1925. One of the most significant turning points was the Easter night of 1925 when Sergei felt an otherworldly joy and again had an experience of the Divine Light he had known in his childhood. The exhibitions and successes he had with his art[115] no longer held the same meaning for him as he became increasingly drawn by the desire to know his Creator through prayer. For this purpose he enrolled in the newly opened theological Institute of Saint Sergius[116] in Paris but found that theoretical studies and the history of the church, however interesting, did not facilitate prayer.

> Inside myself I was torn between art and prayer. After a stubborn, long-drawn-out contest prayer won. Subsequently, in the Theological Institute now, prayer did not help me to concentrate my attention on the subject being taught. … It was a great help to me at the Institute that I was given a room to myself over the professors' quarters where I could pray in my usual attitude. Nevertheless, despite all my interest in the life

---

114. *Letters to his Family,* p. 31.

115. He exhibited at the Salon d'Automne in 1923 and at the Salon des Tuilleries in 1924, which was only by invitation, chosen among the elite of the Salon d'Automne.

116. The Institute of St Sergius opened in Summer 1925 with a preliminary course attended by 24 students. Here he came into contact with Father Sergei Bulgakov (1871-1944). He was also acquainted with Nikolai Berdyaev (1874-1948). See N. Sakharov, *I love therefore I am*, Crestwood: Saint Vladimir's Seminary Press, 2002.

> and history of the Church my spiritual need to dwell in prayer was impaired, and I departed for Mt. Athos.[117]

Sergei arrived on Mt Athos in the autumn of 1925 and entered the large Russian Monastery of St Panteleimon. Here he found the ideal conditions to give himself unhindered to prayer, yet his suffering continued.

> My heart burned constantly. My mind clung to the rock-face, as it were, of God's word. … During that period I trod an invisible rope over bottomless pits. A curious despair would seize me from all sides, like the sea embracing a drowning man. I say 'curious' because when the feeling of despair abated, I was somehow left dying spiritually. Like a volcano this despair provoked ardent prayer.[118]

During the first five years of his life in the monastery he remained full of perplexity over the question of how to live. It was only in 1930, when he met the elder Silouan that his life took another turn. As he related to his family,[119]

> …this unlearned man Staretz[120] Silouan answered the questions which preoccupied me, which no one else had resolved. (And I had been living in Paris at a time when there were very well-respected representatives of the highest Russian culture – in the spheres of theology, philosophy, and general culture.)[121]

St Silouan[122] had lived a similar extreme spiritual life at the edge of the abyss and from the knowledge he had gained was able to explain the various states that Sergei, now monk Sophrony, was experiencing.

117. *On Prayer,* p. 40.
118. *On Prayer,* p. 73.
119. The following passage comes from a talk given to his family in 1975. In 1958, Father Sophrony visited Moscow for the first time since he emigrated 1922. Until then contacts with his family were broken due to the dangerous political situation.
120. 'Staretz' is the Russian word for elder.
121. *Letters to his Family*, p. 33.
122. Silouan was numbered among the saints in 1987.

> The Staretz was unlettered but no one could surpass him in craving for true knowledge. The path he trod was, however, quite unlike that of speculative philosophers. … Christianity is not a philosophy, not a doctrine, but *life,* and all the Staretz' conversations and writings are witness to this life.[123]

The elder, who had gone to school for only two winters, lived a spiritual state of the highest and most rare quality and thus was able to shed light on Father Sophrony's states of despair and prayer.

> In spirit [the ascetic] sees the abyss of 'outer darkness' opening wide before him, and so his prayer is ardent. There is no describing the mystery of this vision or the intensity of the struggle, which may last for years until the heart is purified of all passion, until the Divine light appears which reveals the falsity of our former judgments – the Light which leads the soul to the infinite expanses of true life.[124]

Another question that continued to follow Sergei throughout his life was the question of creativity,[125] "…my previous career naturally inclined me to reflect on creative work in general, and its meaning. …" Upon meeting the elder Silouan it was one of his foremost questions and he finally received the answer to his long searching:

> …where creative work is concerned, in his ultimate search man gradually abandons all that is relative and temporal, in order to attain undying perfection. On this earth perfection, to be sure, is never absolute.

123. A. Sophrony, *St. Silouan the Athonite*, Tolleshunt Knights: Stavropegic Monastery of Saint John the Baptist, 1991, pp. 110-111.

124. *Ibid.*, p. 167.

125. The question of creativity remained a burning question for him, but he addressed it in a different manner during this period, not through painting but through reflection and discussion with his elder. There are a few icons attributed to his hand on Mount Athos, but on the whole he did not occupy himself with painting during his years there.

126. *Wisdom*, pp. 14-15.

> And yet we may call them perfect who speak only what is given to them by the Spirit, in imitation of Christ Who said, 'I do nothing of myself; but as my Father hath taught me, I speak these things'.
>
> This creative work is the noblest of all work available to man. Man sets out, not passively but in a creative spirit, towards this ideal, but always remembering to avoid any tendency to create God after his own image.[126]

Before his death elder Silouan left all his writings to his disciple. After the Staretz' repose, Father Sophrony, who by now had been ordained a deacon, retired to a cave on Mt Athos to live a hermit's life in order to embrace more fully his life of prayer. He lived in this 'desert' during the difficult years of WW2 when Greece was occupied by the Germans and suffered many deprivations. The civil war, which followed straight after WW2, was not less hard and Father Sophrony prayed ardently for peace during these terrible years of war and slaughter. At this time he was also called upon to become the spiritual director of four of the monasteries,[127] and in order to serve this ministry was ordained to the priesthood.[128] He continued however living as a hermit in the 'desert' until after the Greek Civil War when he decided to return to civilization to edit and publish the writings of his elder. Accustomed as he was to life in France, he returned once more to Paris where he brought out a first roneo-typed edition of the Startez' writings.[129] He soon realized however that 'modern' educated people were not able to perceive the profundity of the Staretz' writings, since they were written in a too simple and direct language for them. So he found himself

127. The monasteries were the ones of St Paul, Grigoriou, Simonos Petras and Xenophondos. He also became spiritual father to some of the hermits.
128. His ordination to the priesthood was on the 2nd February 1941, with the prayer to become a spiritual father exactly a year later.
129. The roneo-typed edition appeared in 1948, with the first printed and expanded edition following four years later.

obliged to write an explanatory part to the writings. At about the same time he was in need of a major operation which left him partially invalided making the return to his cave on Mt Athos impossible. He settled in a suburb of Paris where he was able to convert a former goat stable into a chapel in which to hold his services. His strength was greatly diminished and he spent most of it consoling the people who turned to him for spiritual guidance. During this time a group of young men and women had gathered around him wishing to lead a monastic life. Finding himself in a position of responsibility for them, it became necessary to find a place to live. An old unused Rectory was found in the English countryside and Father Sophrony with his small community moved there in 1959. Throughout all this time, though he was busy building and establishing his monastery, the prayer did not slacken, he was forever searching for a closer and fuller relation with Christ, the *Being.*

> The touch of Divine love in the heart is our first contact with the heavenly side of the abyss.[130]

In England, where life became more settled and stable,[131] Father Sophrony found himself again able to take up painting. All through his years of searching, the question of creativity had been one of his preoccupations, how the Creator created. Having now found the true *Being,* Christ, and having learned to know Him as a person, establishing a living contact with Him through prayer and ascetic life, Father Sophrony had arrived at a state where he could turn to art again. This time though, art was not a means to search for the solution of the problem of *being,* but to try to express what and Whom he had learned to know, the True *Being.*

---

130. *His Life is Mine,* p. 62.
131. In France the group had lived in scattered accommodations and would only really meet for the services.

> When we receive His grace we also have the gift of creativity; we become co-workers with Him in our re-creation, in our refashioning and regeneration. When we receive this grace our heart is enlarged to embrace heaven and earth and to bring every creature before God, that is, to spread the creative energy of God and the blessing of God over all creation.[132]

He found himself in a position where he could explore how to represent his Creator and to do this he took up icon painting. Yet, he soon found out once again that the means at his disposal were inadequate to attain the unattainable. Every icon of Christ only – at the most – contained a fraction of the Person, yet he did not despair or give up, but kept persevering, because now, in this new form of art, there was hope of representing even this fraction, and every fraction was getting one step closer.

As his biographer[133] stated,

> "For him, creation is another word for hope."[134]

132. *Man the Target of God*, p. 250.

133. Rosemary Edmonds (1905-1998) translated Father Sophrony's books into English, and was also instrumental in purchasing and donating the property of the Old Rectory in Tolleshunt Knights to him for the foundation of his monastery.

134. *His Life is Mine,* Introduction, p. 13.

CHAPTER 4

Painting true *Being*

FATHER SOPHRONY ARRIVED IN England on the 5th of March 1959. He was accompanied by a few others from the group who had gathered round him in various accommodation in his vicinity of Saint-Geneviève-des-Bois, a suburb of Paris. He had lived there the previous 12 years and had built a small chapel in which to hold his church services. Now in the quiet English countryside some friends found a rectory in vacant possession which they were able to purchase and it became known as the Old Rectory. Here a more organized monastic life was possible for the small community but Father Sophrony did not think he would live very long having always suffered from poor health and only partial recovery from his extensive surgery. In fact he was to live for another 34 years and see his monastery grow beyond all hope and expectation.

So started the new period in Father Sophrony's life. It turned out to be a rich and creative time, with unexpected results.

> From the very beginning we could get busy with the creation of a church inside the house, which we finished (not completely, but the main work) towards the end of he sixth week of Lent. Already for Holy Week and Easter I celebrated in it. We are now thinking of enlarging it a little more, which is quite feasible, and then our little chapel will be really beautiful.[135]

The reception room which was enlarged to include the former entrance hallway was chosen for this purpose and when the icon-screen, brought over from France was installed, their chapel became deeply loved by all.

Once this was completed, Father Sophrony's next priority was to build an icon studio. He had painted a few icons while on Mount Athos,

135. *Letters to his Family,* p. 83.

and possibly also in France, but now he thought the time had arrived to occupy himself more fully with this work to convey visually all that he had found and learned during his lifetime. As a young man he had felt constrained to give up his painting in order to strive for a fuller knowledge and contact with Him whom he was seeking; now he sought to depict this same Person in paint. The most suitable means for this was the iconography[136] found in the Orthodox Church. He had lived with and studied the wall paintings and icons on Mount Athos, becoming familiar with the different schools and varied styles developed over the centuries. He had contact with icon painters who had shared their model drawings with him, so although he did not produce many icons himself, he had nevertheless been studying the work in depth. In France he had made friends with several iconographers, notably Father Gregory Krug and Leonid Ouspensky, both of whom had painted several icons for him at his request.[137] He had also encouraged some of his monks to study with Ouspensky and would for several years contact him about technical questions that arose during his work. So after several decades of laying aside his painting, Father Sophrony was now prepared to take up again his former profession.

> However strange it may appear, despite the fact that I am already an old man, and have not worked as an artist for 36 years,

136. Though the term 'iconography' carries broader meaning than just orthodox sacred art, we shall throughout use this term to describe just this.

137. Leonid Ouspensky (1902-1987) and Monk Gregory Krug (1908-1969) both belonged to the icon painters of the Russian emigration in which the position of icons was both special and creative. As the need for icons and frescoes arose, the painters of the emigration turned to icon painting. Some of these painters had been part of the revival of the icon which took place in the early years of the century, when icons were restored, taken out of their natural environment to be put in exhibitions and seen for the first time as works of art. However, other painters of the emigration had never been involved in anything to do with icon painting before. The result of this new engagement in icon painting was the creation of a new school of iconography which was freed from several of the superfluous aspects that had crept into the tradition in Russia. Refreshing and 'life-giving' qualities emerged in the icons from this new school.

> I see that this 'vein' has remained alive in me. What I am seeing once more in myself was in its time the cause of my totally forsaking painting. It is impossible to be divided inwardly to such a degree. If you want to do something, let's say something that could be 'bearable', inevitably one's full attention must be devoted to this work, which stands in contradiction to the other quests of my soul. But we shall see what God disposes.[138]

As a painter he knew the best requirements for an ideal art studio and set about creating one suitable for the task. For this the foundations of a former pigsty on the premises was used, and the structure of the building was a henhouse from a neighbor, but raised on several courses of bricks to give a good height. Part of the roof was glazed to give an even light from above which facilitated taking advantage of the most suitable light angles as the work could be moved around inside.

Another reason for building the studio was the idea that icon painting could provide a source of income for the community. On Mount Athos the smaller brotherhoods often lived from this work. Father Sophrony would test the gifts and abilities of every member joining his community, to see who would be capable of this work. Quite soon however, the small monastery was discovered by some families from London and people started coming for the services and to seek advice from Father Sophrony. This gave surer provision for their livelihood, but even so, the icon painting was never abandoned and both Father Sophrony and some of the brethren worked on commissions[139] as well as painting the icons needed for their own use, in the chapel and monastery. Though iconography was the best means to express what he sought, Father Sophrony soon realized that perfection was not attainable even in this form of art. In writing to his sister about an icon he had just painted, he comments,

---

138. Letter of the 15th June 1960, *Letters to his Family,* p. 93.

139. The icon commissions came both from individuals as well as from other churches.

> It is superfluous to write that I am only partially satisfied [with the icon]. The work of an iconographer is very poorly paid. But I altogether prefer to do a good icon for a minimal price than to accept a lot of money for a bad piece of work.[140]

The painting of icons turned out to become more of a service to the people, than providing a means of living.

Although Father Sophrony had received a traditional academic[141] art training, painting portraits and still-lifes, working mainly in oil, his youth had also coincided with the most experimental and creative period in Russian art history. He himself had spent some years working with abstract art and had keenly observed everything that was produced and painted around him. However the technique of egg tempera was new to him and he studied it diligently, trying to follow all the practices of traditional orthodox iconography.

He describes it in a letter to his sister Maria,

> I have not written to you for a long time because I am positively drowning in my 'duties' towards the people who look to me. Apart from that we are, of course, still obliged to earn our crust of bread by our labour, and in addition, to share it with others. One of the ways we earn our living is by painting icons. After the great influx of people during the summer was over and it became possible to retreat into the studio, I spent two months painting icons. One of them is large in size: 152 cm. by 194 cm. Icons on wood of such dimensions are historically rare. There have been icons of greater height than two metres, but then the width was smaller. But of this width together with such a height there have been few in the history of icons. It is hard to

140. *Letters to his Family,* p. 193.

141. Recent research has shown that Fr. Sophrony did not study at the St. Petersburg Academy of Art, but received an equally classical art foundation in the private studios that he attended.

Archimandrite Sophrony, early 1960s.

> paint them according to the canon of iconography, that is, using paints dissolved in egg-yoke. An icon must be in a horizontal position, and furthermore, as perfectly level as possible. But now is not the time to speak of this technical side. I was to some extent satisfied with the result. After a break of forty-five years, to solve an exceptionally difficult [artistic] problem was not a simple matter. Now we have a whole stream of orders. I'm afraid to, as it were, return to my past. That is, once again to be totally preoccupied with 'art', leaving everything else.[142]

Though he had not been painting for so many decades, the artist was still very much alive in him. This is clear from his writings, where he frequently uses painterly metaphors and observations. It was natural for him to return to the mode of expression with which he was most familiar in order to convey his knowledge and experience. His earlier art training helped him in more than one way. The knowledge he gained in his earlier art training which included composition, the theory and relationship of colour, texture and knowledge of the human figure and more especially the face, all now came to serve in his work of iconography. While he made use of all these techniques himself and taught them to others, he emphasized that his more classical academic[143] way of painting was not to be copied. He urged his followers to study traditional iconographic techniques, saying that his own roots were steeped in the academy, and were not an example to be followed, as any external copying would be false.

ICON PAINTING

In iconography he found a fulfillment of the various techniques he had learned, even the abstract, since the icon, if seen in its details, is composed of abstract components: the garment, mountains, to a

142. *Letters to his Family,* pp. 190-191.
143. This teaching he is likely to have received at the studio of F. Rerberg.

certain extent buildings and even faces, carry aspects of abstract art. These abstract components, though not visible or noticeable without a closer study, form an essential part of the icon, giving it its strength and structure.

Mountains in icons are like abstract art. But in iconography this abstract art has a meaning.[144] Without the abstract and constructive detail the icon starts to resemble renaissance art, to which it is both closely related and at the same time far removed. In renaissance art the main point is on overall line and composition, while the icon has a close and intricate inner structure. In the former the main emphasis is on expressing a feeling or mood, while the latter concentrates on the inner purpose. These differences can be observed in all the details of the two styles, both in technical details as well as in the treatment of the subject matter. The aim of the icon is first and foremost to inspire prayer, while renaissance art aspires to express the sublime and aims more at emotion than prayer.

It was not only in the compositional aspects that abstract art proved to be useful, but also in its technique and principles of design;

If one looks at a drawing in an abstract way, then one sees pictorially in the shapes where there is need of lines and colours to give a general balance.

However, a sound knowledge of reality was needed and he would encourage serious study of anatomy and nature. *Know the anatomy and then you can make deliberate mistakes,* because, *even to copy one needs knowledge of anatomy.*

From his earlier training in classical academic techniques, he knew how to analyze and understand the difference between icons and naturalistic art, knowing what to follow and at which points to depart;

---

144. All quotes in italic are from the author's notes of oral discussions with Father Sophrony.

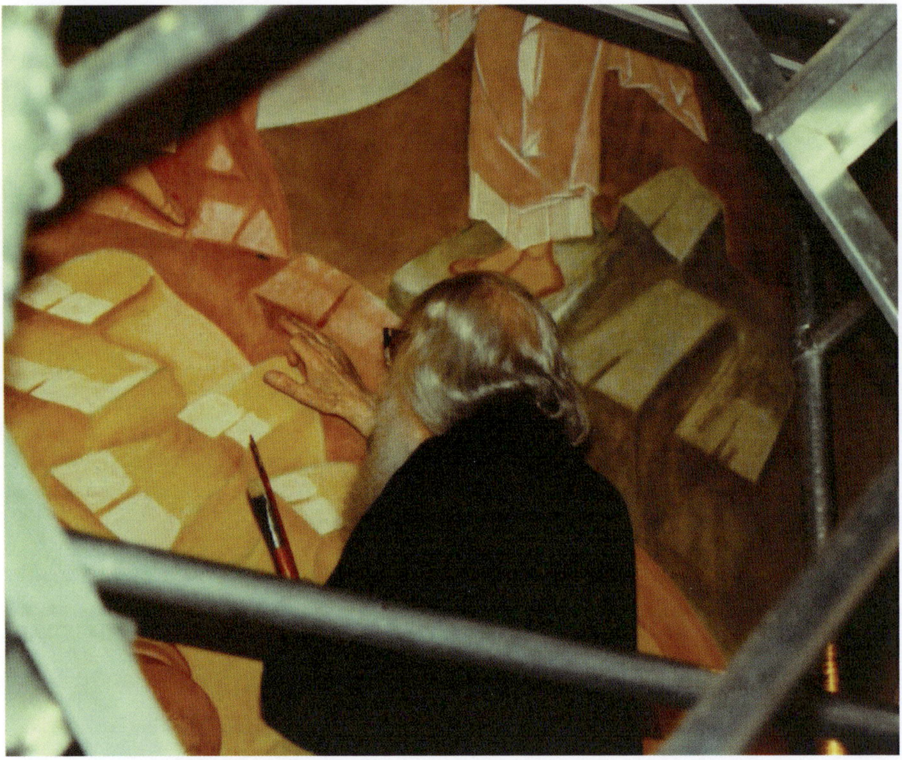

Fr. Sophrony painting the mountains on the Transfiguration mural,
Monastery of Saint John the Baptist, Chapel of Saint Silouan, 1985.

You have to follow the hand's classical measures and then throughout adopt some special 'style' even if you copy from different places. He meant that one should work out a pattern of stylization after having studied the various ways in which it can be done. Having decided upon a particular stylization, there was a total freedom of expression.

Hands in icons don't have to be naturalistic, the main thing is that there is harmony in the icon. It is rare that one finds beautiful hands in otherwise beautiful icons. With a solid knowledge of the principles of stylization, the details were of minor importance in relation to the whole. The main aim was to create beauty with harmony and calm, which was to be attained by a freedom of creation, where anatomical and naturalistic detail could be ignored.

One has to work like a sculptor, follow the lines of the body, first for the drawing, afterwards for the light. All lines should follow the movement and the light too.

Although the light on garments was often created in an abstract shape, frequently in a fashion of crystals, the general distribution of these components had to follow the anatomy of the body underneath, comprising both abstract and figurative art. However the objective was to avoid too much naturalism.

If an icon does not have wrong proportions, it is not an icon any longer.

THE FACE

The most important aspect of the icon for Father Sophrony was the face, as the face reflects the person's inner life. As a professional painter, after his period of abstraction, he had earned his living as a portrait painter. He had learned to observe faces and characteristics, *when I was a painter I could paint a portrait of a person if I had only spoken with them for 10 minutes.* This knowledge was then changed into another sense of awareness, *but since I stopped being a painter I don't even realize what people are wearing. But I see (feel) their spiritual level – and recognize, remember people.* Even formerly as a painter, this aspect, of portraying the inner essence of the person was not altogether foreign to him, as it was traditionally a common striving among all Russian artists to try to capture the soul of the person painted. How to depict the soul remained a problem for them all, some managing better than others. However, the phenomenon of the person remains a mystery, but many artists explored this question and expressed it in various ways. The person is depicted on the face, by the face; the face reveals an echo of the soul. Florensky writes in his work "The Pillar and Ground of the Truth", regarding old Russian painting, that the devil does not have a face, but is painted without any features, without any expression, as a non-person.[145] Kazimir Malevich (1879-1935), the creator of the black square, which in itself was an icon of an icon, at a certain period of his life, painted figures with heads in the shape of eggs, without any facial features whatsoever. Yet he was said to be a believer. Filonov, on the other hand, who declared himself to be an atheist, always started his paintings by depicting an eye, and would move on from there, painting the whole face.[146]

The language of icons offered Father Sophrony another and new way to render the soul and the inner person. The icon captures all the eternal aspects in its stylization, and thus also touches upon the inexpressible. He remarked that, *even the most ugly faces become beautiful with grace.*

A contemporary artist has expressed the same understanding,

> To represent sanctity requires the capacity to contemplate the eternal in the temporal, to reveal the invisible through the visible… Simplicity, majesty and light emanate from the faces, which are calm with a penetrating look.[147]

It was precisely the eyes that carried the most importance, as they would reflect the inner man, the soul. Father Sophrony had several thoughts on how the eyes were best represented, and developed a style of his own. He preferred to give a calm and interior look to the faces he painted, letting the eyelid cover part of the iris and touch the upper part of the pupil, thus avoiding a too direct and an intensely focused look. He never added any light inside the pupil, which is often done in naturalistic painting, because he considered that this gave an evil look, the pupil should be fully black and calm, not having light as if from within.

145. P. Florensky, *The Pillar and Ground of the Truth*, Princeton: Princeton University Press, 1997, p. 504.
146. Cf. *Experiment Vol. 11*, Los Angeles, 2005, p. 241.
147. H. Bléré, *Lumière Joyeuse,* Bruxelles: Racine, 2014, p. 17.

The expression of the eyes should be simultaneously both interior and exterior; the eyes should look at the onlooker and yet be fixed within. *In order to express an eternal gaze it is good to paint the eyes focusing slightly apart, i.e. a little bit wider than parallel,* which gives a broader, farther and at the same time an all-encompassing look. He also liked the eyes to express a certain sadness, which he said is a natural consequence of looking at us, at the world and at the state of things.

The severity is in the eyebrows, as is the suffering, sadness, which is what one often sees in frescoes. A great artist paints sad eyes, but the rest normal and calm. Thus no drama but an inner tension, which is calm, yet still expressive and dynamic.

It was also important to him that a measure of sobriety was kept.

Beauty is when the same colour is everywhere in the face, not a bit of yellow, a bit of pink etc, that the face had a base colour of a single tone throughout whereupon the modeling was built up. He held strongly to the artistic principle of a restricted colour palette, keeping a controlled harmony and thus ensuring that the colours worked well together, creating a calm whole. He emphasized that the stylization of the faces should be moderate, not too exaggerated, neither too expressive, nor too stylized, but it was essential to keep an aspect of beauty in them.

The faces must not be too naturalistic, yet still stay human and not be over transfigured.

It is important that an icon should have a presence in order to depict a real person and be someone one can turn to and relate with. *When one paints a saint one learns to know him or her.* This relation to the icon is essential for its later use, as a focus of prayer, but equally true at the moment of painting and he would advise, *When you paint, pray to the icon you are painting (Christ, the Mother of God, martyrs…) – ask them to help you, iconography isn't an easy work.* It was also important not to

Mother of God (detail), early 1960's, monumental size icon, Monastery of Saint John the Baptist, chimneybreast in the study of the Old Rectory.

treat it as a dead task but remember continually that one is dealing with real, alive persons and needing to ask for their help and guidance.

Always pray when you paint! Pray that we may see, learn to know Christ. Pray to St John the Baptist that he helps us to see Christ – he was the greatest among the prophets because he was the first who knew Him.

Though ideally in the portrait the scale must not be greater than reality, in icons Father Sophrony preferred to use larger dimensions, much larger than life-size. In the early years of his career as an artist he painted several works of monumental size. These sometimes demanded technical solutions, which he took advantage of in his later work on icons. Soon after arriving at the Old Rectory he painted a large icon of the Mother of God for the chimneybreast of the study. Here there was not enough distance to view the icon properly, so he resorted to foreshortening and adapting the features in order to look in proportion from the sitting position at the desk opposite.

He liked to paint the Mother of God. Once he had painted a large icon of her which he was able to finish in just one sitting. It happened that this icon turned out to be the perfect size for the icon screen of Saint Silouan's chapel, built many years later, and all the other icons were modeled on its size. In this icon Father Sophrony painted a large dark deep shadow line all along her face, which gave both depth and seriousness while also introducing a stylization. He did not like her icons to be too sweet:

My icon of the Mother of God is strict but with a mildness as well. A dark shadow on the cheek line can give a good effect. It was better to avoid soft modeling, which easily gives a sweet and soft expression as did the use of red in the colour palette. He preferred her to be serious.

Another important aspect in the faces is that they should have presence and not be made weak by having the base colour too transparent. As the icons are painted from dark to light, presence is given by a solid base having a certain matter while the building up of light can be done with varying degrees of transparency.

The expression of the face is of first and foremost importance while the other traits and proportions can be sacrificed to serve this. Stylization of the features lends itself to a freer interpretation of the face and person and natural restrictions do not have to be followed.

We should make the faces of the icons attractive, so that the onlooker is able to pray. The icons should be like a springboard towards eternal life.

THE ICON AS A PORTRAIT

When Father Sophrony's elder, Staretz Silouan was numbered among the saints, it became necessary to paint his icon-portrait. In the case of a person of whom one has photographs it is surprisingly more difficult to paint an icon. The photograph captures the external aspects of the person's likeness, while the icon represents both the external and more importantly the internal side as well. Yet, it is important to have a model to work from, as: *No artist can paint many portraits of faces before they start to look like himself.* In his book about Saint Silouan, Father Sophrony had 'painted' a portrait of him in words, not only of his physiognomy, but also in a theological aspect.[148] When it came to painting his icon, he based it only partially on the photos, explaining that the photo shows the person in a split second, while the expression of a man of prayer changes every second, depending on his inner state. He was unhappy with the few photos that had been taken during the Staretz' life time, because they portrayed a hard face, while in reality he had a soft and gentle look. He tried to depict this combination of outer likeness and inner state. For the iconographic identity, that is those particular features by which the person depicted in an icon may be recognized, Father Sophrony chose

148. *"I drew a portrait of Silouan when I spoke about the theology of the person – the hypostasis. It is a point which is not easily realized and which cannot be reached through human strength on its own."* (Talk to the Community A-16, unpublished).

Saint Silouan, 1988. Monastery of Saint John the Baptist,
Chapel of Saint Silouan, iconostasis.
Mark Edwards, info@markedwardsphotography.com

to represent his elder with two black streaks in the beard and a strong vertical line on the forehead. The outline of the figure did also play an important part in conveying the overall expression, both the outward appearance with his exceptional strength and his inner humility and meekness. This was achieved by a modification of the shoulder line and the width of the outline of the head.

TEXTURE

The surface of a work was of primary importance to Father Sophrony. The surface of a wall painting should be totally matt to prevent any reflection so that the work might be viewed from any angle. *The surface is very important, not to the touch, but for the eye. The surface of an icon is like porcelain.*

This was a subject he had learned in his youth, when the question of *faktura* (texture) was a burning issue.[149] It was discussed and experimented with by all, in every field of art, even extending to sculpture, typography, poetry, music and the performing arts. The most important aspect for Father Sophrony was that the surface should have a "culture" and "nobility", meaning by this that if it is worked to a perfect state it will reflect upon the entire work which will then emanate a nobility that is felt unobtrusively and yet becomes the hallmark of a masterpiece.

In this respect, someone whom he valued highly was Rembrandt, not only for his masterly treatment of light and the spiritual quality of his portraits, but also for his treatment of surface, especially in the backgrounds. Rembrandt felt that the light surrounding an object or person carried as much importance as the subject being painted. Describing his impression in his own words:

149. The topic had been popular with many artists and critics in Russia in the 1920's, notably Punin, Markov, Kruchenykh and Tarabukin. Kandinsky lead a debate on this with Rodchenko at the Inkhuk discussion group, see Khan-Magomedov, S. O., *Rodchenko: The complete works*, London: Thames and Hudson, 1986.

> I noticed that … it was an object surrounded by a whole lot of different sorts of air – all of which were of a different texture … The light in front … was different from the light behind it, which was different again from the light on the left of it and all these different sorts of light did not remain the same, but changed every moment. Of course, when I say 'light' I mean air and when I say 'air' I mean light … then the idea suddenly struck me … does all this space – this air- really have a color in our sense of the word and is it possible to translate that color into terms of paint? … from that moment on … I have been convinced that every object in the world is surrounded by a substance (call it light or air or space or whatever you like) which somehow or other it must be possible to express in the terms of light and shade and half a dozen of primary colors.[150]

This unique understanding and rendering of light was Rembrandt's finest achievement. He paid as much attention to the surrounding of a figure as to the subject itself. In doing this, he found a way to model space and time and as a result his paintings have a profound stillness. His portraits have the same quality, the rendering of a moment in eternity while being illuminated as though from within.

> When we artists look at a work of art, we concentrate on the external characteristics of color, form, technique, and so on. When we look at a Rembrandt, all this fades into the background before the impression of its inner content and the human, spiritual element of the person depicted.[151]

On the whole Rembrandt was a painter before his time; the Russian painters valued him highly because of his acute insight

---

150. H. W. Van Loon, *The Life of Rembrandt van Rijn,* New York: The Heritage Press, 1930, pp. 222-226.

151. Leonid Pasternak, *Autobiographical Fragments,* Experiment Vol. 1, Los Angeles, 1995, p. 38.

and understanding of all the questions and problems for which they themselves sought solutions. Rembrandt himself knew very well that his own contemporaries did not understand his vision:

> Heaven forbid that I should ever see things the way they do! … Any one can learn to paint the things that are there. But to paint the things that one merely suspects to be there while one can't possibly prove that they are there – that is the sort of task that makes life interesting.[152]

COLOUR

Father Sophrony also paid great attention to colour, its interrelations and effects. He knew which colours would enhance one other, which would complement and those which would cancel each other out.

To see the values of the colours, one has to see them all together. Be brave and paint colours – it also depends on the surroundings if they work or not.

He was equally conscious of the importance of the proximity of tone and outlines. Sometimes the garments were constructed through the interplay of adjacent colours, volumes and shapes.

Learn to see what goes, what fits together and what doesn't. Let your eye see and decide on its own and then check the thing with your brain. He was concerned to maintain a creative and non-determined relation to the work; *When I paint, I try things out.*

He would treat each icon as a work of art, again partly abstract, so as to judge its colour effect and design in an open and unbiased way. He advised:

152. *Life of Rembrandt*, p. 226.

If something doesn't go, colourwise, one changes what is next to it, so that the effect becomes different, in order to preserve an overall harmony in the colour and to keep the general composition together, colours had to be modified. He warned however the work would never be easy or straightforward; *There is a war between lines and colours – they are rebellious, they always want to become wrong. To be able to solve all this is a great experience.* He always urged his collaborators to stretch themselves beyond their natural boundaries, to develop further their senses and abilities. *Learn to compose with colours and lines, as when one plays the piano.*

When I was young I did not like lines. The painters used colours and shapes which played against each other, these then determined the dividing lines.

This latter method reflected his earlier training which had been influenced by the Russian Cézannist school where lines as such were avoided being rather made up visually by the juxtaposition of two colours in their various form. In this way the work had more volume, it was neither just graphical nor flat. In his icons Father Sophrony tried to do the same, bringing a painterly quality into them. An illustration of this was the unusual way he painted the garment of one of the figures on a wall painting depicting the Entrance to Jerusalem. He used a light green undercoat and modeled the shades of the garment on top of this in red ochre, working in the reverse manner normal to iconography,[153] but the result was very effective, in spite of this reversal. He commented on it: *The garment of the first figure in Jerusalem is not bad. The style is a bit cubist and a bit like Rublev.* The term 'not bad' signifies the second highest form of praise in the colloquial language of Sergei and his friends at the time, the highest epithet being 'not bad at all'. In the comparison with both Rublev and cubism, one can see a great freedom

153. The norm in orthodox iconography is to work from dark to light.

of approach, an uninhibited and creative attitude of feeling able to use whichever style was most appropriate for the subject.

ICONS AS ART

Father Sophrony considered that although the iconographical canons are strict and somewhat rigid, one should be able to lift them out of the area of being just a craft. *One must arrive at painting the icons as works of art.* That is to say that it was incumbent upon the artist to paint beautiful icons, not just traditionally correct ones, or simply copy existing icons.

When you make an icon, don't copy exactly. Not because you can't do it as well as the original, but because it is already done, it is in history, already consecrated, one mustn't repeat. He thought it essential to keep a creative attitude, always moving onward and forward. *We must come to the state of painting icons with our personalities inside.* Meaning by this, to give oneself entirely to the work, putting oneself fully into it, yet at the same time respecting its form and content, not imposing one's own ideas, but rather becoming co-creators together with the icons.

> *Art has something that can help one to come nearer to the first Artist. As curious people used to look behind my back at what I was painting when painting in plein-air, so, in the same way, it would be good to be able to stand behind the back of God and watch Him creating.*

In all art, but especially in icon painting, the artist is not always fully in control of what happens and the work sometimes takes on a life of its own.

Imagine, here we make a few lines and a few colours and we make what God has created. When this happens the painter feels he is just collaborating with what is growing of its own accord. *When an artist paints or draws he cannot really control what is happening, it is something external that directs it.*

However there are some occasions when it may be necessary to copy something, in which case this also should be done, with an open and positive mind, as Father Sophrony describes; *An artist who copies something CAN make a masterpiece,* meaning that a copy does not have to be bad; it can on rare occasions turn out even better than the original.

Every detail has to be carefully measured and considered, *The difference between a masterpiece and a banality is a matter of a few millimeters.* A good work can very easily be ruined by the wrong touches and once ruined is not easily put right.

Father Sophrony felt that another danger within iconographic tradition was that archaic by-gone styles could become fossilized by the attempt to repeat exact copies. As expressed by one of his contemporaries: Exact replicas…

> … of archeological objects are right for museums, but not for art [because a relationship of] this kind with the object also ruins it as a historical creation, turning it into something incredibly boring for the public.[154]

Father Sophrony would stress that contemporary people could not feel the same as the inhabitants of Byzantium and hence the severity of expression had to be modified to be more accessible to modern man.

We are not born in Byzantium, we cannot artificially see like the Byzantines did

It is not normal for us to do as they did.

154. Nicholas Roerich (1874-1947), Quoted by Nicoletta Misler in "Dance, Memory! Tracing Ethnography in Nicholas Roerich", in *A Feast of Wonders, Sergei Diaghilev and the Ballets Russes,* (Exhibition catalogue), Berenice: Skira , p. 76.

Resurrection, Christ, (detail), early 1980's. Wall painting, Monastery of St John the Baptist, Refectory.

He thought that icons should to a certain extent be allowed to evolve, in order to adapt to the needs of contemporary people and be an inspiration for them rather than an historical object. This whole question of evolution in iconographic tradition is of course a very delicate matter. Father Sophrony would carefully test every new idea with much prayer and careful thought before putting it into practice. In the case of the murals in his monastery, he found that the gentle and diffused light that exists in southeast England needed a special colour scale, softer and more subtle than the colour combination that could be used in Greece with the hot sun and strong light, and again even that which was suitable to be used in Russia where the northern light differed in quality from that of Essex. He did not follow any particular style or school, but took what he thought would be useful from each. When questioned about this he suggested a way to respond: *When people ask what style we paint in say: 'it is not Byzantine, it is not Greek, it is not Russian, not English, not..., not..., not..., but it is not bad!'*

And adding, *In 100 years, if the world still exists, then they will see as we do and understand us.*

His main concern was always for the expression and the artistic effect that the finished work would have. The artist in him was still very much alive.

ABSTRACT ART

Father Sophrony had learned stylization and abstraction in his youth from the work of Cézanne and the Russian artists who followed him. He had also studied pure painting and total abstraction under the influence of Kandinsky. Pure abstraction proved to be a very useful knowledge in the painting of icons, as the lines, colours, movements and interrelations follow the same principles.

Having much experience in this field he had also faced its problems and pitfalls as he related,

> *During 2 years I was obsessed about the idea to* ***create*** *something. I met an artist who had painted a picture with different yellows on a blue background. I asked him what it represented. The painter said it was a tree during a certain season against a blue sky. A little later I went to the exhibition of this painter and saw the painting hung upside down. The artist explained that he had tried to hang it in all directions. I then understood that one cannot draw a single line without the help of God.*

This realization became a determining factor in breaking free from abstraction. Upon realizing there was no line, shape or colour that did not already exist he turned instead to seek their Creator, abandoning the futile attempt to create something new himself. Father Sophrony was once asked if one thinks when doing modern art; his answer was: *"Yes, but as when one wants to squeeze out some old mustard from a tube. One thinks with the eyes."* What he implied by this was that the creation of abstract work has a forced quality, like the difficulty of getting old dried up mustard out of a tube, which needs both patience and perseverance. The best way to overcome this is by not thinking, but rather allowing the eyes to judge the situation in a non-intellectual, purely perceptive and visual manner. Picasso was of the same opinion:

> The idea of research has often made painting go astray, and made the artist lose himself in mental lucubrations. Perhaps this has been the principle fault of modern art. Those who paint after ideas paint the invisible and, therefore, the unpaintable.[155]

At one point, in 1983, two punk youngsters came on a study visit to Father Sophrony's monastery to look at icons. They asked Father Sophrony why he had left painting, to which Father Sophrony replied:

155. C. A. Tsakiridou, *Icons in Time, Persons in Eternity*, Burlington: Ashgate, 2013, p. 285.

When I was a child I spoke like a child, I thought like a child. When one is a child one does what one thinks is best to do then – it is later that one discovers what is more important, and then one leaves the other. When I was young I was dreaming of dying with a paintbrush in my hand. Thanks to God that I did not die then!!

On another occasion some Greek artists visited the monastery and asked father Sophrony the same question: why he had left painting and become a monk. This time he gave a more enigmatic answer:

In art there is nothing, that is why I became a monk. Or like a musician from the Bolshoi Theatre who went to the countryside to have a rest and there he saw a man with a violin who sat on the threshold of a house watching the main road of the village and played and sang the whole day: "One donkey cooomes, anoooother dooooonkey coooooomes, the fiiirst doooooonkey leeeaveees, the seeecond dooonkeyyy etc, etc etc", the whole day. The musician from Moscow told him that those who play the violin in Moscow play fast, move their fingers, searching to find better harmonies, better sounds, why did not he do so? His answer was: "They are still searching, that is why they play like that, but I have already found it."

After having related the story, he added for the benefit of the younger painters to whom he had been speaking:

So, you understand: to have found something and to say that everything else is wrong, makes that all that is right become wrong. Measure with the eye. If it wants to stay, if it becomes happy over what it sees, then it is good. Apart from that, pray, read, love people.

And adding:

When I am dead study around you, look at the world, look at examples and learn.

Here he meant that one should never relax and think that the solution is found, but always strive on, searching for a fuller, deeper and truer way to express the art.

MURAL PAINTING

With time, as the monastery expanded and more people came, a hall was built and this was the first time Father Sophrony could create monumental size art again. There is no mention that he studied this technique in his youth, but his knowledge of mural art and composition points to the fact that he must have had some experience in this genre. He enlisted the help of several members of his community instructing and advising them on the art of mural painting. However he always put the freedom of the person above the work. He insisted visiting artists be given 'carte blanche' when doing parts of a design or painting, in order to persevere their own creativity. This followed Kandinsky's teaching that true art could only be created if there was freedom.

COMPOSITION

Father Sophrony used various aspects and techniques from his knowledge of constructivism and special composition when designing the interior of St Silouan's chapel.[156] In order to create a visual dome, which he had not been able to build, he designed a series of concentric circles in the middle of the ceiling on a background of gold. Under these hung a chandelier also circular which echoing the ceiling brought a dimension of depth. Over the sanctuary he created a visual vault with semi circular lines which on the east wall were reflected in the curtain overhanging the Last Supper and mirrored on the table surface. The movement is then picked up by the embroidered tapestry carpet in front of the Holy Table. In this way he combined and bound together

156. This was the first purpose built chapel in his monastery. The wall paintings were started in 1983 and the chapel was consecrated in 1988.

not only the walls and ceiling, but also the space in-between, creating a 4 dimensional composition filled with dynamic inter-relation.

The overall effect of this which purposely is not obvious at first glance, gives a feeling of wholeness, welcoming and encompassing the visitor, producing a sense of eternity by uniting the historical Last Supper with the timeless image of the heavens into one and the same composition, without any line of division. Father Sophrony gives here a visual image of his concept, from *being* to *Being,* from the terrestrial to the heavenly, from the temporal to the eternal - where time has ceased to exist.

In the composition of icons he drew on the rich inheritance of his earlier education, adding the constructive element to the underlying structure. The constructivists had initially been inspired by the icon's simplicity and clarity of line, using it in their own creations. Their work concentrated on dynamic lines, an aspect that proved useful to re-introduce into the icon where it had been partly forgotten due to overemphasis on detail and technical perfection. Father Sophrony strove to achieve an inner unity in his iconographical compositions, with a continuity of line and echo of form, devoid of superfluous detail.

The lines of a drawing should have continuity, be reflected in nearby lines and shapes, to bind the composition together in an unobtrusive yet palpable way. He would say, *For drawings: search for an equivalent, do not repeat the same lines.*

This is a practice used by Rublev, but also later, in post-revolutionary Russia by the constructivist artists, who were working during Father Sophrony's formative years and whose influence he could not avoid, as we have seen above in the lay-out of St Silouan's chapel.

When composing icons with mountains or other scenery for their background, he emphasized that the colours should be used in a way

East wall and ceiling, Monastery of Saint John the Baptist, Chapel of Saint Silouan.

Idem with lines of dynamic movement highlighted.
Photograph by kldphotography.co.uk

to build up the whole, not be put on flat without any thought of the interrelations and effects on each other.

In nature it is not as we are doing it, painting dark next to light etc. but that is how one sees it. Also in normal painting one arranges the things. As he had learned during his plein-air painting time at Barvykha; *You have to observe nature. This does not mean turning yourself away from God, but to learn technique by observing His creation and learning from it.* This is reminiscent of Kandinsky's urge to his students to observe nature in order to gain inspiration to create something new and abstract, for in nature may be found solutions to line and colour and all aspects of painting. In composition likewise, *Sometimes one has irregularities which can be helpful as it gives life, but on other occasions it is not desirable.* Yet, *It is important to have a harmony, nothing distorted or unbalanced, but in details there must not be any repetition, no mirrored hand, eye etc.* The composition should be measured out carefully, like a poem where no word is either lacking or superfluous.

In icons, and generally everywhere it has to be just right, not too much and not too little. Everything should be measured to perfection. This it is hoped will create an inner vibration in the spectator.

Here, once more, we find a parallel with Kandinsky's thought:

> The beautiful corresponds to the inner, emotional necessity. The beautiful is inwardly beautiful.[157]

LIGHT

Another value of great importance was the rendering of light.

Light is one of the attributes of God, he often reveals Himself through light. Father Sophrony had encountered this in early childhood when he contemplated two kinds of light:

---

157. *The Life of Vasilii Kandinsky* p. 100.

> There were occasions when coming out of church I would see the city, then the whole world for me, lit by two kinds of light. Sunlight could not eclipse the presence of another Light. To think of it brings back the feeling of quiet happiness that filled my soul at the time. I have forgotten almost all that happened in that period of my life but the Light I have not forgotten.[158]

From these early experiences of the Divine, or Uncreated Light, all through his childhood Father Sophrony was continuously fascinated by the fathomless depth of the blue sky and would lie on his back contemplating the 'bottomless' blue of the sky. In his mature years, as a monk on Mount Athos, the fascination was still there. But this time it took on another, further dimension.

> I would look up at the clear blue sky, sometimes staring fixedly in one direction, at others letting my eyes sweep from one edge to the other. When my gaze reached the horizon, I would travel further and mentally embrace our whole planet. I would peer into the depths, trying to penetrate its boundaries; but the longer I stayed my attention on the marvelous scene – the more eagerly I studied the heavenly sphere, full of light – the more the mystery fascinated me. And when, by a gift from on High, it was vouchsafed to me to behold the Uncreated Light of Divinity, I saw the blue sky of our planet as a symbol of the radiance of heavenly glory. This radiance is everywhere – filling all the depths of the universe, ever intangible, *other*-worldly for the created world. Azure-blue is the colour of transcendency.[159]

In Father Sophrony's youth the subject of light was a burning fascination. The recent invention of electricity, which became widely used, was a novelty as indeed the discovery of x-ray, exposing internal structures

158. *We Shall See Him*, p. 37.
159. *We Shall See Him,* p. 166.

and organs of living things was a cause of wonder. The uncreated light however shows another reality, a spiritual, otherworldly reality.[160]

Light in icons is often rendered by transparency, and sometimes by gilded surfaces. It was this that Father Sophrony used in Saint Silouan's chapel: the light was reflected off the gilded ceiling, which bathed the whole atmosphere in a golden light, maybe in order to try and recreate the otherworldly light he had experienced as a child when coming out of church. The other way to represent light is by the juxtaposition of light and darkness. This is often used in icons to set off the light and emphasize the divinity of Christ by encircling Him with concentric circles of blue, the innermost of which is nearly pure black. The darkness expresses the notion that God Who is unknowable may not be represented.[161] However, Father Sophrony on the whole preferred the positive aspects of representing Christ and concentrated on these.

An example may be seen in the icon of the Transfiguration, where Christ is standing in a circle of these concentric spheres, dressed in white, Father Sophrony gave not only white garments but an outline in white which enhanced the effect of luminosity and transparency.

EXPRESSING TRUE BEING

Father Sophrony's reason for painting icons was first and foremost in order to find an expression to represent the true *Being,* Christ. The icon with its language of stylization and emphasis on the interior life, was the most appropriate to convey what he had learned and found.

Writing to his sister, he expresses his thoughts:

> I have been forced by the work on icons itself to plunge into the depths of past centuries. I have been thinking about those artists,

---

160. The uncreated or Divine light is often described and represented by concentric circles of various shades of blue.

161. The source of this aspect is apophatic (negative) theology. See p.133, footnote 195.

Preparatory drawing of Christ, mid 1980's. For wall painting of the Resurrection, Monastery of Saint John the Baptist, Chapel of Saint Silouan.

> spirit-inspired iconographers, who strove to express, in the material flesh of the ICON, the union of Uncreated with created. Some of them intentionally 'distorted' the human face, using this means to tear the mind of the person praying away from the earth, so as to transfer it to a world of another dimension. Others, while holding essentially the same views, sought the connexion between the image and the Prototype and expressed *both dimensions*, i.e. the temporal and the eternal, in human features. But they have transfigured these human features, and they never allowed themselves to descend as far as naturalism, which the Western painters in the age of the Renaissance did not escape.
>
> It is relatively easy to create an image pleasing to the eye by a hint, by a sketch. But exceptional genius is needed to 'complete' a work without sinking into 'carnal beauty'. The wonderful history of the Icon knows many master-artists; some of them preferred to violate all the proportions or traits – others, such as St Andrei Rublev, created an exceptional harmony of two worlds in works of a rare completeness. I like both the first and the second. But the second stand higher in my estimation as true spirit-inspired artists and masters.[162]

Father Sophrony chose to strive towards the aim of Andrei Rublev, uniting the human, the otherworldly and divine, to create icons that are both beautiful and stylized while at the same time, expressing the eternal.

> ... the power of the icon is truly a transfiguring power, especially in our century, when this spirit has been lost, when the feeling for beauty has been lost, when the very notion of 'beauty' has become vague elusive.[163]

---

162. *Letters to his Family,* p. 192.
163. *Letters to his Family,* p. 179.

One way of depicting the other worldly divine Person of Christ is by reflection, that is to say in the expression of those seeing Him. Commenting on the calm expression of St John the Baptist in a Deisis[164] icon, Father Sophrony said; *When we meet our Creator we cannot look as calm as St John looks now. I tried to paint it on the face of Adam in the refectory.*[165] Here he is referring to the mural of Christ's descent into hell where in the wall painting of the resurrection, Adam meets his Creator again after many centuries of separation. His expression is a mixture of love and shame, awe and wonder; his eyes are wide open in disbelief and happiness.

Adam (detail), early 1980s. Wall painting of the Resurrection, Monastery of Saint John the Baptist, Refectory.

164. Deisis is a composition where Christ is in the centre in a frontal pose, with saints flanking him either side turned towards him in supplication.
165. The refectory referred to is the first building in his monastery where he first painted murals, built and painted in the late 1970's until the early 80's.

Moses receiving the Law, (detail), 1985, Preparatory drawing.

Moses receiving the Law, 1985. Private collection.

MOSES

Moses has always been a key figure for monks and ascetics as can be seen in the canon of St Andrew of Crete:

> Moses, the great went to dwell in the desert,
> seek to follow his way of life, my soul,
> that in contemplation thou mayest attain
> the vision of God in the bush.[166]

Father Sophrony felt very close to Moses, as someone who had shared the same thirst and search for the meaning of *being*, as he himself had. He was grateful to Moses, through whom mankind had received the first revelation of "He Who Is"[167] – the Divine *Being,* un-originate and personal.

---

166. Andrew of Crete, *The Great Canon,* Canticle 5, verse 10. Translated by R. Edmonds, unpublished.
167. *Exodus*, 3:14.

Moses receiving the Law, 1985. Private collection.

> To Moses belongs the undying glory of having brought mankind closer to Eternal Truth.[168]

Father Sophrony painted two icons of Moses where he tried to express the wonder, awe and love with which the revelations inspired the prophet. These were in the encounter at the Burning Bush and the Receiving of the Tablets of the Law.[169]

In the receiving of the Law, the icon is given expression by the composition, which is diagonal, a thrust of movement towards the top corner where the two tablets of stone are handed to Moses. The whole attitude of the prophet is full of attention, respect and reverence. The face expresses both love and fear. [170]

In the icon of the Burning Bush,

> Moses is speechless, he is looking with intensity... The Bible says nothing of the prophet at that moment, only of God, how He began to speak from the burning bush. But we know that Moses lived, as did other prophets, in that attentive desire to see God as He is. He was searching for an answer to the question "What is this existence? Wherefrom is it? Who is the cause of it?" and so forth. And, being man, he could not form the right notion of God. But the Lord revealed to him: "I am that I AM", in response to his prayer.[171]

---

168. *is Life is Mine,* p. 18.
169. In both cases he followed a 10th century Byzantine illumination as his model, where Moses is depicted without a beard, see E. Bacalis, *Identity Crisis: A Portrait of Moses in Byzantine Art,* MA thesis in Late Antiquity and Byzantine Studies, King's College London, 2003, unpublished.
170. It is unusual to paint faces in profile in icons. Since one cannot have eye contact with a face in profile, evil figures are often represented in this pose. However, there are exceptions, the 10th century miniature mentioned above is one of them. Here the main focus is on the moment of the receiving of the law, so Moses is facing the hands giving him the tables of stone and could not be represented in a three quarter pose.
171. A. Sophrony, *Dukhovnye besedy*, tom 2, Moscow: Palomnik, 2007, p. 153.

CHRIST

The most important and essential question remained: How to portray Christ - true *Being* - Whom he had come to know through his long intense search and struggle.

The fact that Christ was a person, fully attainable and – as such – depictable, only partly facilitated the problem. As both perfect man and perfect God, both natures had to be represented. The divine, naturally, cannot be depicted, and to try to do so brings a danger of falling into sentimentality, yet to concentrate on the fully human side may equally have the same result. The stylization of the icon leant itself to a more 'detached' image, which could hold together the two aspects of human and divine. Father Sophrony knew that it was impossible to attain to a full and correct representation, and that each icon at best could only catch a small fraction of Christ. To paint the perfect icon was beyond human means.

However he never tired of trying, and made countless drawings and sketches for the many icons and murals on which he worked, always striving to draw nearer to his goal. Some icons he would repaint over and over again, adding details, shadings, altering the face colour with glazes and adding or removing some millimetres of the outline, because the silhouette also contributes to the overall expression.

He considered that the strict Byzantine murals of Christ were not fitting for our time, being too strict and severe for modern people. He sought instead to portray Him in a gentler form, tending towards a consoling and merciful expression which he thought would speak more to contemporary man. He was greatly helped by the discovery of the Turin Shroud,[172] which he considered was a particular gift

172. The shroud which traditionally is considered to be the burial cloth of Jesus Christ has certain vague markings depicting a ghostly human figure. In 1898 the Italian photographer Secondo Pia, when developing a photograph of the Shroud, saw that the negative of the photo represented a fully recognizable human face. As such he discovered that the vague markings on the Shroud were 'negative' and when reversing the markings by the photographic process, these markings became 'positive' and readable.

Christ in Glory, 1974.Welling, Church of Saint Michael.
Reproduced with the kind permission of the Rector of St Michael's Church.

Seraphim Angels: Details of *Christ in Glory*, 1974. Welling, Church of Saint Michael.

Reproduced with the kind permission of the Rector of St Michael's Church.

for our century. Although, as mentioned earlier, it is not necessarily useful to have a photograph as a model when painting icons of people, nevertheless the 'photo' of Christ which the negative image of the Shroud presented, helped as an inspiration and indication of how to portray Him. Father Sophrony would keep a copy of the Shroud next to him when painting the face of Christ, but explained that it could not be followed exactly, as the cloth had been draped on top of the head, and therefore had some irregularity in its proportion when stretched out flat. However, it was a great source of inspiration and together with the stylization of the icon, it helped to produce a face which was both human and at the same time portrayed the Divine aspect.

One of the commissions Father Sophrony was given was to paint a large icon of Christ in Glory for an Anglican parish where the altar painting had been destroyed during the war. The large frame was empty and he was asked for an icon to be painted to fit it. The work gave scope for Father Sophrony's wide experience and skill and he sought as far as possible to create an image worthy of the subject. Christ is clothed in white with golden ochre lines of folds and pure white highlights. He is seated on a throne which has strong constructivist roots in its shape, layout and components, giving a special effect through its curves and angles. Behind there are geometric shapes, some in flat colour, others filled with either line drawings or lightly modeled figures. The shapes are reminiscent of suprematism and the rays of light which emanate from Christ are also dynamic and directional, broken where intercepting other shapes and continuing after the fraction with equal strength. The overall colour harmony is strong and bold, giving a convincing and dominating presence of glory and majesty, yet the expression on the face of Christ is both mild and approachable.

Although ultimately it is not possible to render a full likeness of Christ, yet the icon may be compared to a 'spring-board' from which one may rise towards the real Person.

Holy Trinity, early 1980s. Wall painting,
Monastery of Saint John the Baptist, Refectory.

> Contemplating the ikon of Christ, in spirit we rise into contact with Him. We confess His manifestation in the flesh – He is both God and man, wholly man and perfect Divine likeness. We go further than colours and outlines into the world of the intelligence and the spirit.[173]

THE HOLY TRINITY

Another possible way of representing true *Being* was through Rublev's icon of the Trinity, the adapted scene from the biblical Hospitality of Abraham, but where Abraham and Sarah are removed, leaving only the three angels.[174] This icon is "an icon of an icon" in so far that the three angels that visited Abraham only represent the Trinity, as the Father and the Holy Spirit did not take on flesh and as such are not strictly speaking paintable.

This is an icon that shows the utter humility and unity of the three Persons, expressing the mystery of the Divine *Being*. The three angels are seated in harmony and in total dedication and deference to one another. The humility of the three persons is indescribable, inexpressible and unattainable. The construction of the icon is circular with the dynamics of the circle moving from one person to the other, in a silent and still harmony of love.

Father Sophrony held this icon in deep respect considering it to give a profound lesson without need of explanation. He felt it should always have the central place when designing a place of worship. In the refectory, which was initially to be used for services, he painted it opposite the main door, as the main central focal point. He followed Rublev in the layout, omitting Abraham and Sarah, so as to emphasize its deeper meaning, rather than just representing the historical scene. He did however change the colouring used by Rublev, dressing the side

173. *On Prayer*, pp. 166-7.
174. *Genesis* 18:1-15.

angels in white, partly to emphasize their state of not being incarnate and also for the purely artistic reasons of strengthening the colour composition of the mural. The two side angels have a band of colour, a cloth, draped over their legs, each repeating one of the two colours of the central angel the effect of which creates a triangle within the circle.

The inscription on the icon shows that it is a presentation of the Pre-Eternal Council[175] in which the creation of man is decided, "Let us make man in our image, after our likeness" (Gen 1:26). Man – created with free will in the full knowledge of the risk of his falling away from God.

> *One of the Trinity asked:*
> *"What if man falls?"*
> *The Son, the second person of the Holy Trinity, answered:*
> *"Then I will go and save him."*

THE LITURGY

It was one of Father Sophrony's foremost priorities to make a chapel worthy and appropriate in which to celebrate the Liturgy, the meeting place between God and man. He had several designs and ideas about how to create such a space and though he had quite a few places of worship during his life, it was only with the chapel of Saint Silouan that he managed to create a place specially designed for the Liturgy.

> The Liturgy embraces in itself all our life; in the Liturgy are included all the levels of our being in its turning towards God. The Liturgy, as long as it is lived with all our being, enables us to live it as a truly Divine Act, which not only bears within itself this visible world in its entirety, but also goes beyond this world's limits to an infinite degree.[176]

175. This expression of the Trinitarian divine will is associated with the idea of a 'Pre-eternal Council', partly with reference to Is. 9:6, where some Septuagint versions have the phrase 'the Great Council'. Cf. *Letters to his Family,* pp. 72-73, footnote 91.
176. *Letters to his Family,* p. 71.

Father Sophrony painting the face of Christ at the *Last Supper,* early 1980s.
Monastery of St John the Baptist, Refectory.

The chapel of Saint Silouan took several years to complete. Father Sophrony himself worked on the wall paintings, assisted by several of the members of the community.

> *It is something very important what you are doing: to paint a church – the Divine Liturgy. Do it with fear and don't judge yourselves as unworthy, do NOT work with negligence, because what you do now will have consequences later on.*

He painted what he could himself and supervised the rest, deciding on drawings, designs, colours and treatment of surfaces. Several ideas and thoughts were tried out and changed if proved unsuccessful.

> Humanly speaking it is impossible to put together in one and the same space all the combinations of form and colour. The attempts of our past artist-theologians to gather together a 'theological summa' expressed in colours, frescoes, have led to an incredible perfection that nothing later has surpassed in beauty.[177]

A whole hearted attention was given to produce a space worthy for the Liturgy with nothing left to half measure. The ceiling and sanctuary have already been mentioned, but in addition the use of contrasting gold and bronze on the ceiling, upon which large white seraphim angels were painted, further enhanced the dynamic movement. These circular movements have an effect of drawing the visitor into the scene, embracing him in the timeless space created by the whole composition. The walls were painted with murals in a continuous sequence, without dividing lines, giving another timeless quality. The colours, mainly pastel tones were gentle and serene, yet with an underlying seriousness. Prime importance was given to the texture and surface which was totally matt. All the furnishings, wood paneling and carpets received equal attention and were carefully measured so as not to detract from the murals, but rather enhance them. Vestments and textiles were made specially

177. *Ibid.*, p. 137.

to blend with the whole, adding their particular tone and colour. The lighting posed more of a problem but after a lot of effort, finally the best solution was found by reflecting it off the gilded ceiling which created a golden non-directional light adding yet another dimension to the space.

All was carefully tempered to be harmonious, calm and peaceful.

Throughout the entire design, Father Sophrony created, as far as possible, a perfect place for the meeting of man with God, *He Who is Being.*

> I AM THAT I AM. Yes, indeed, it is He Who is Being. He alone truly lives. Everything summoned from the abyss of non-being exists solely by His will. My individual life, down to the smallest detail, comes uniquely from Him. He fills the soul, binding her ever more intimately to Himself. Conscious contact with Him stamps a man forever. Such a man will not now depart from the God of love Whom he has come to know. His mind is reborn. Hitherto he was inclined to see everywhere determined natural processes; now he begins to apprehend all things in the light of Person. Knowledge of the Personal God bears an intrinsically personal character. Like recognizes like. There is an end to the deadly tedium of the impersonal. The earth, the whole universe, proclaims Him: 'heaven and earth praise him, the sea, and everything that moves therein' (Ps. 69.34). And lo, He Himself seeks to be with us, to impart to us the abundance of His life (*cf.* John 10.10). And we for our part thirst for this gift.[178]

178. *His Life is Mine*, p. 26.

Last Supper, Christ, (detail), early 1980s. Wall painting,
Monastery of Saint John the Baptist, Refectory.

CONCLUSION

Father Sophrony's icons, way of painting and thoughts on iconography are highly personal. They reflect his unique path of development rooted in the Russian avant-garde of the 1920's, passing through an intense period of spiritual search which lead him to Christ and culminated in him expressing all he had found in paint. However this is not to say that his icons cannot be of inspiration to others; showing an opening to something further; open a window to a new view. His offering to the icon is to bring things back to the essential, to give a minimalistic message, concentrating on what matters: the person, both the one depicted on the icon and the viewer, inspiring a living relation between them.

> In [Archimandrite Sophrony's] prayer two realities are connected: the living God and the actuality of earthly life. In like manner, in painting, the idea of penetrating divine eternity through the contemplation of visible reality prevailed in his conscience.[179]

179. From a manuscript by Fr. Sophrony where he sketched down his thoughts for an introduction of *His Life is Mine,* unpublished archive, in Russian.

APPENDIX A

Members of the 'Bytie' group

Elena Fedorovna ANASOVA (1901-?) Studied in the studio of Konchalovsky at VHkUTEMAS, participated in the plein-air painting trip to Barvikha in 1920, did not become a member of the Bytie group and did not exhibit with them.

Zoia Nikolaevna BOGOIAVLENSKAIA (1899-?) Studied drawing, from 1918 at Svomas/VKhUTEMAS in the studio of Konchalovsky. No further information after the plein-air painting trip to Barvikha.

Leon (Levon) Mikhailovich BOUNATIAN (1899-1972) (later know as Leonardo Benatov[180]) Born in Kağızman in the district of Yerevan in Armenia, at the time under Russian rule. Moved to Tibilisi in 1909, followed evening art classes until 1914. Moved to Moscow in 1915, studied first in the studio of Milman and Miganadjiyan, and from 1916 with Mashkov. Shared a workshop with Rodchenko and Smirnov in 1917, through whom he came into contact with constructivism and abstract art. In 1918, enrolled in Svomas/VKhUTEMAS in 1918, in the workshop of Konchalovsky, where he remained until 1922 when he emigrated to Paris. Founding member of the 'Bytie' group. Participated in the first and second exhibition of Bytie in 1923. Married the daughter of Philippe Maliavin, Zoya. Second marriage with Norwegian novelist, Liv Ingeborg Olsen (Livja Flood). Exhibited widely, among others at the Salon d'Automne and Salon des Tuilleries.

Anatolii Adrianovich LEBEDEV-SHUISKIY (1896 or 8-1978) Painter and graphic artist. Born at Shuya. Studied under Korin in Moscow.

180. His name was changed to this as he registered in France. In order to be consistent throughout this book, his 'French' name shall be used in the texts, except where there is a quote from a contemporary source.

Worked at the studio of Kelin in Moscow 1916-1918, after which at VKhUTEMAS with Konchalovsky and Archipov until 1924. Member of the Society of Moscow Artists (OMKh), with whom he exhibited from 1918 onwards.

Nikolai Pavlovich RAZHIN (1892-1942). Studied at the Studio of Mashkov from 1912. Conscripted into the army in 1914. After demobilization returned to Mashkov's studio, which by then had moved to VKhUTEMAS, where he studied until 1922. In 1929 became member of AKhR (Association of Artist of the Revolution).

Sergei Semeonovich SAKHAROV (1896-1993) Born in Moscow. Studied at private studios, possibly Rerberg and Mashkov. Enrolled at the Svomas/VKhUTEMAS in 1918 in the workshop of Konchalovsky. Served in the army as an engineer officer in the camouflage division in 1913-1917, again in 1919 and 1921. Founding member of the 'Bytie' group, exhibited in first exhibition January 1922. Emigrated in 1922, travelling through Italy, Berlin reaching Paris end of 1922. Exhibited at Salon d'Automne in 1923, and Salon des Tuilleries in 1924. Gave up painting, enrolled in newly opened theological Institute of St Serge in 1925 in Paris. Autumn 1925, left Paris for Mt Athos, Greece, where he entered the Monastery of St Panteleimon and became a monk in 1926. Ordained deacon in 1930. Encounter with Saint Silouan in 1931 with whom he had close contact until the latter's death in 1938. Ordained priest in 1941. Left Mt Athos in 1947, returned to Paris to publish writings of St. Silouan, which appeared in 1948. Lived near Paris until 1959 during which a small community gathered around him. Moved to England in 1959 where he founded the Community of St John the Baptist. Painted icons and wall paintings. Wrote and published several books. Reposed there in 1993.

Alekandrovich Pavel Petrovich SOKOLOV-SKALIA (1899-1961) Painter, illustrator, graphic artist, painted posters, also worked in the theatre. Born near St Petersburg, in 1906 moved to Saratov and in 1914 to Moscow. Studied in the studio of Mashkov from 1914 to 1918 and at VKhUTEMAS from 1920 until 1922, again with Mashkov and also with Manganari. From 1926 member of AKhRR (Association of Artists of Revolutionary Russia). Later in life painted historical genre paintings in social realist style, posters and illustrations. Received several medals for his work.

Grigori SRETENSKIY (1899-1972). Born in Moscow, studied at the Moscow Spiritual Seminary and then history-philology at Moscow University. From 1918 until 1924 at VKhUTEMAS in the studio of Konchalovsky. Shared a studio with Sergei at Borby square. After the departure of Benatov, he was the main organizer of 'Bytie'. Participated in all their exhibitions until 1927. Married a fellow artist and student of Mashkov, Nina Stenshinskaya (1901-1988), in 1923, who also became member of Bytie and exhibited in all subsequent exhibitions. Continued to work in the Russian Cézannesque style, exhibited in many other exhibitions.

Aleksander Alekseevich TALDYKIN (1896-?) Studied with Konchalovsky at VKhUTEMAS. Active 1921-1929. Theatre designer, painter. Represented at the exhibition "Art of Moscow Theatre 1918-1923" held in 1923.

MEMBERS OF THE FIRST 'BYTIE' EXHIBITION:

Leon Mickhailovich Bounatian (1899-1972) - Konchalovsky.

Sergei Semenovich Sakharov (1896-1993) – Konchalovsky.

Anatolii Adrianovich Lebedev-Shuyskiy (1896 or 8?-1978) – Konchalovsky.

Grigori Aleksandrovich Sretenskiy (1899-1972) – Konchalovsky.

Aleksandr Alekseevich Taldykin (1896-) – Konchalovsky.

Pavel Petrovich Sokolov-Skalya (1899-1961) – Mashkov.

Nikolai Pavlovich Razhin (1892-1942) – Mashkov.

(Names behind dates denotes which teacher they studied with)

GROUP GOING TO BARVIKHA

Elena Fedorovna Anasova (1901 - ?)

Zoya Nikoloievhiya Bogoiavlenskaia (1899 - ?)

Leon Mickhailovich Bounatian (1899 - 1972)

Anatolii Adrianovich Lebedev-Shuyskiy (1896 or 8 -1978)

Sergei Semenovich Sakharov (1896 - 1993)

Grigori Aleksandrovich Sretenskiy (1899 - 1972)

Aleksandr Alekseevich Taldykin (1896- ?)

APPENDIX B

The abyss, asceticism and theology

FATHER SOPHRONY'S SEARCH FOR *being* was, as we have seen, the 'leitmotiv' of his life. He journeyed along many and varied dramatic paths which initially led him far away from the *Being* for whom he searched, yet he never entirely lost the trace of Him.

> If he did anything in any sense good, he did it through the remnants of the primitive goodness of his will. By the fall of man into sin, the image of God was broken in him, but neither entirely demolished nor destroyed; the eternal Sun was setting in his soul, but its last rays are still glowing on its heights.[181]

His searches led him to an abyss, to the edge of the unknown, from where there was no turning back.

> It is more difficult to ascend a height, than to fall into an abyss.
> Is it therefore better to fall into the abyss?[182]

He came up against an impasse which only a leap into the unknown could resolve. He took that leap of faith by which he found the long desired fulfillment of his search in the meeting face to face with his Creator, the true *Being*. He understood that what he had been longing to know was revealed as a Personal God.

> Abyss of wisdom, O Christ,
> Treasure of knowledge and personified goodness…[183]

His leap of faith brought him not only safely across the abyss, but to a height from which he viewed that which surpassed his every hope and

181. Metropolitan Philaret of Moscow, *On the Necessity of the Incarnation*, in *Select Sermons*, London: Joseph Masters and Sons, 1873, p. 248.
182. *Ibid*, p. 137.
183. Menaion for 10th January, Canon of matins, ode 1, tone 5.

imagination. His life took wings, like the eagle, who…

> …flies high in the clouds and scans remote horizons with its sharp eye, catches from afar the scents of the earth and delights in the world's beauty; knows many lands, seas and rivers, and beholds a multitude of wild beasts and birds.[184]

This is the realm of the man who has come to know his Creator,

> Apprehending the depths of the Creator's wisdom, we embark on the suffering through which Divine eternity is to be attained. And when His Light shines for us we unite in ourselves contemplation of the two extremes of the abyss – on the one side, the darkness of hell, on the other, the triumph of victory. We are existentially introduced into the province of Uncreated Divine Light. And hell loses power over us.[185]

Now there was no further question of an abyss of darkness and of non-being, but rather a new endless horizon lay before him; the abyss had been transfigured by light. In the words of St Philaret of Moscow:

> Shall I strive to raise your souls from the earth, to carry you above the sun and stars, to transport you into the heaven of heavens, past the lower and higher order of Angels unto the extreme heights of creation, thither where time is not, for there eternity reigns intransient and indivisible, where space is lost in infinity, and where by a retrospective glance you may be convinced how little exaggerated, how feeble even is the saying of the wise Solomon, "that the whole world is before God as a little grain in the balance, as a drop of the morning dew that falleth down upon the earth". (Wisdom 11: 22)[186]

---

184. *St Silouan*, p. 496
185. *On Prayer*, p. 170.
186. Mtr. Philaret, *Select Sermons*, pp. 92-93.

THE CREATOR AND CREATION

After the discovery of the Personal *Being,* God and Creator, the remaining part of Father Sophrony's life was spent in obtaining a fuller and deeper knowledge and contact with Him. One of the paths to which his quest had led him was the artistic one which in turn brought him to iconography.[187] In this he strove to portray an evermore true and faithful presentation of the *Being* whom he had come to know and love.[188]

> Having in the beginning made man without collaboration on the part of man, God has never since done anything with man without enlisting his co-operation. The natural world is so arranged that man is constantly faced with problems to which he must seek solutions. But in order truly to work with God in the creation of the world man must ever aspire to the utmost possible knowledge of God Himself. The continual climb towards further and further knowledge of God is also a creative act, though of an especial order.[189]

God has endowed man with absolute freedom which may be used in any way for different purposes. With this freedom he has also given man the ability to create whereby his freedom might find fulfillment. This is reminiscent of Kandinsky's method of teaching (see Chapter One, pp. 14-15), which presupposed a total freedom of the student in order to be able to create any abstract work. It is similar in the case of God's gift of freedom to man but which goes much further: in the creative act of striving for a fuller knowledge of the Creator, man arrives at a more complete awareness of his creative work and in so doing draws nearer to the Creator Himself. As Father Sophrony in his youth had been preoccupied with the question of creation, of the relation of the person to creativity and the evaluation of art, this

---

187. The term 'iconography' is used as a synonym for 'icon-painting' all through this chapter.
188. For a full study on the concept of *Being,* see A. Zacharias, *Man, the Target of God.*
189. *Wisdom*, p. 13.

question now started to take on new dimensions. In the past he had searched for the meaning of *being* through art, while now he realized that the way to true creation was by approaching the Creator, the *Being*, himself, and through closeness to Him, the question of true creation was resolved.

> The mental state […] of the artist creating a work of art […] cannot be compared to that of the man of prayer brought face to Face with the living God.[190]

> I was filled then with reverent worship for the First Craftsman, the Creator of all things, and a longing to meet Him, learn from Him, know how He created.[191]

Creative activity finds various modes of expression. The highest of these is prayer, pure contemplation of the Creator, sometimes inspired by the view of His Creation. Other creative work may be expressed as man explores his potential and finds himself stretched beyond his normal boundaries.

Startetz Silouan[192] helped him to understand the deeper meaning of creation:

> My talks with Staretz Silouan concentrated, of course, on prayer and living according to God's will; but my previous career [as a painter] naturally inclined me to reflect on creative work in general, and its meaning. … Talking with the Staretz fixed my attention on the Person of Christ: how did He, the Son of man act? … It is proper to man to aspire to perfection, to wish to

190. *His Life is Mine*, p. 55.
191. *Wisdom,* p. 14.
192. Father Sophrony related how none of the professors he had met in his youth had ever spoken so surely and simply about the truth as Silouan had. Cf. A. Sophrony, *Eikodomontas ton Nao tou Theou,* Vol. A, Tolleshunt Knights: Stavropegic Monastery of Saint John the Baptist, 2013, Talk Nr 18, pp. 228-239.

> enter into the living stream of divine eternity whither the Christ-Man was the first to go.[193]

Having found his Creator and true *Being* the question of eternity and creativity was partly solved but took on another dimension. This was how as a painter he was to depict his enlarged vision. It was an inevitable need for the artist to want to express himself once more through painting.

One way in which the undepictable, is revealed is through the image of light. The uncreated light, which,

> "by its nature is absolutely different from ordinary physical light. Contemplating it begets, first and foremost, an all-absorbing feeling of the living God.... In spirit he [man] beholds the Invisible, breathes Him, is wholly in Him.... Faith is light, but in small measure. Hope is light but not yet perfect. The perfect light is love"[194]

The uncreated by its very essence and nature cannot be rendered in created form, therefore it needs to be represented in a stylized and symbolic way. The symbol for transcendence is blue and in order to depict the Divine which is ultimately unknowable and unattainable for man, iconography employs a formula for rendering the uncreated light by use of a circular or oval shape. This is made up of concentric circles in different shades of blue which get darker towards the middle, becoming almost black in the inner central part. This middle space represents the inexpressible and the unattainable mystery, the presence of God. The tradition of painting the Divine presence and uncreated light as darkness has its origin in apophatic theology,[195] which argues

---

193. *Wisdom,* pp. 13-14.
194. *St Silouan*, pp.171-2.
195. Apophatic theology emphasises the absolute otherness of God and His character beyond cognition and utterance. It concentrates on the aspects of God that are not and cannot be known and as such is often being described as "negative theology", tending more towards philosophy.

that since God is unknowable, He can only be known and represented in darkness or in 'nothingness'[196]. There are interesting parallels between this form of theology and abstract art, where fullness is also portrayed by a negation of the form.[197]

Yet, darkness is not the only way that the other-worldly light is represented in icons. Father Sophrony preferred the positive aspect of both theology and the rendering of light with emphasis on the known aspects, instead of the unknown. In Father Sophrony's student days at the Theological Institute of St Serge in Paris, the apophatic theology of St Dionysius the Areopagite was widely known and appealed to many because of his emphasis on the darkness and the unknowable mystical aspect of God. Initially Father Sophrony was drawn to this way of understanding but later turned to concentrate on the positive aspects of contact with God and His love.

In the icon,

> The light in particular no longer falls *on* the figure from outside, but streams out *from within it,* and surrounds it. This is the light or glory of the divine presence in which the saint stands and which he or she also carries within as indwelling grace – hence the icon as depiction at once of the eschatological transformation of souls and body, and of the mystical experience available in the present life.[198]

As icons are painted from a dark foundation upon which is built light, they appear to emit light from within and thus lend themselves to the expression of the otherworldly and uncreated. The sense of

---

196. See also Chapter Four, pp. 103-104.

197. For a detailed study, see: Anna-Maria Papadaki, *I Apokalipsi tou Pnevmatos: Apofatiki Theologia kai Aferetiki Techni,* Doctoral Thesis University of Thessaloniki, 2010. (http://www.didaktorika.gr/eadd/handle/10442/20443)

198. Alexander Golytzin, "Christian Mysticsm Over Two Millenia," in Basil Lourié and Andrei Orlov (eds.), *The Theophaneia School: Jewish Roots of Eastern Christian Mysticism* (St. Petersburg, 2007, p.xxx.) Quoted in *Icons in Time, Persons in Eternity*, p. 28.

transparency and reflection of surfaces, was also something explored by the avant-garde in Father Sophrony's younger days and which he continued to explore in his iconographic work.

There is a school of iconography which concentrates on rendering the uncreated light, expressed through transparencies and often using blue as a highlight on garments and mountains. Theophan the Greek (1340-1410), one of the icon painters who brought his art to Russia, was a follower of this movement. He, in turn, instructed Andrei Roublev (1360-1430), who became one of Russia's best iconographers and a master of transparent painting techniques. His icons express an otherworldliness in their delicate, yet strong stylizations, the fine traits of faces juxtaposed with daringly abstracted garments, all marked with the same tone of calm and serenity.

While a monk on Mount Athos, Father Sophrony had learned the practice of the hesychastic prayer, known as prayer of the heart. This form of prayer was especially developed in the 14th century by St Gregory Palamas, (1296-1359), who developed a school of theology of uncreated light and prayer.

This form of prayer is directly linked with the apprehension of *Being* in that it is centered in the heart, the meeting place between God and man.

The heart, which is the hidden deep centre of man, is capable of reflecting the image of God like a mirror, depending upon its state. The purer the heart, the clearer and more luminous is the reflected image.

> Our heart must always be crushed by the precepts of Christ, by the grace of God, because just as an image can be imprinted on soft warm wax, in the same way, the image of Christ can be imprinted in a soft heart.[199]

---

199. A. Zacharias, *Tears the Healing of the Person,* unpublished talk.

> …if an artist gives beauty to the world, the artist of artists makes the universe shine with the beauty of beauties. Yes, there is nothing more beautiful than a person who, in the mysterious darkness of inner work, has withstood the murk of sinful alarms and, illuminated, reveals the Divine image, shining like a precious pearl, in himself.[200]

As one practiced in hesychastic prayer, Father Sophrony's custom was to fix his gaze on the face of Christ, but now and then cast a glimpse down at the earth only to return with greater fervor to look again at the face of his Creator.

> In the Jesus Prayer we keep repeating the Name of Christ as if we were filing off rust which we have accumulated in this world, so that this material which is covered with rust may become shiny again, so that we may shine again. If we file off the rust we have accumulated in this world, then that primordial gift of God which we received at our creation will increase, will develop and it will save our souls, that is to say, it will bring us to a full likeness with our Creator. [201]

The icon is inseparable from theology, but it is not always necessary to have theology first. As Father Sophrony told the author:

> *Later, when you paint icons, take Ouspensky's book[202] and study theology. Because we need to know theology. The most important is to follow Christ's commandments. You will come to theology through the icons, it will be like a crown on the work.*

---

200. P. Florensky, *The Pillar and Ground of the Truth*, Princeton: Princeton University Press, 1997, p. 165.
201. A. Zacharias, *Tears the Healing of the Person,* unpublished talk.
202. L. Ouspensky, *The Theology of the Icon*, Crestwood: Saint Vladimir's seminary Press, 1992.

Christ in Glory, (detail), 1974. Welling, Church of Saint Michael.
Reproduced with the kind permission of the Rector of St Michael's Church.

Bibliography

Antonova, I., *Unknown Konchalovsky*, Moscow: Axiom Graphic, 2002.

Avtonomova, N. and Sarabianov, D., *Vasilii Kandinsky. Chronology, 1916-1921*, Experiment 8, pp.3-14.

Bolotina, I.S., *Il'ia Mashkov*, Moscow: Sovetskii khudozhnik, 1984.

Bowlt, J. E., *Russian Art of the Avant-Garde, Theory and Criticism, 1902-1934.* Revised and Enlarged Edition, London: Thames and Hudson, 1988.
— and Washton Long, R. C. ,*The Life of Vasilii Kandinsky in Russian Art, a study of On the Spiritual in Art,* Newtonville, Mass.: Oriental Research Partners, 1980.
— and Misler, N., *Unchartered Territory: Vasilii Kandinsky and the Soviet Union,* Experiment vol. 8, Los Angeles, 2002, pp. 15-21.

Douglas, C. and Lodder C., *Rethinking Malevich*, London: The Pindar Press, 2007.

Experiment vol. 1: *The Russian Avant-Garde*, Los Angeles: Institute of Modern Russian Culture, 1995.

Florensky, P., *The Pillar and Ground of the Truth*, Princeton, N.J.: Princeton University Press, 1997.
—*Beyond Vision, Essays on the Perception of Art*, ed. Misler, N., London: Reaktion Books, 2002.

Kandinsky, *Complete Writings on Art*, translated and edited by K.C. Lindsay and Peter Vergo, Boston, USA: Da Capo, 1994.
—*The Primary Elements of painting 42 (Extracts),* Experiment vol. 3, Los Angeles, 1997, pp.161-168.
— *On the Spiritual in Art (1920),* Experiment vol. 8, Los Angeles, 2002, pp. 59-115.
— *Workplan for the Visual Arts Section of the Academy (Theses),* Experiment vol. 3, Los Angeles, 1997, pp. 157-160.

Kemenov, V.S., *Konchalovsky,* Leningrad: Aurora Art Publishers, 1973.

Khan-Magomedov, S. O., *Rodchenko The complete works*, edited by Vieri Quilici, London: Thames and Hudson, 1986.
—*VHUTEMAS. 2 vols*, Paris: Editions du Regard, 1990.

Lapshin, V.P., *Khudozhestvennaia zhizn' Moskvy i Petrograda v 1917 godu*, Moscow: Sovetskii khudozhnik, 1983.

Lebedev, P.I., *Bor'ba za realizm v izobrazitel'nom iskusstve 20kh godov*, Moscow: Sovetskii khudozhnik, 1962.

Lobanov, V.M., *Lebedev-Shuiskiy*, Moscow: Sovetskii khudozhnik, 1960.
—*Pavel Petrovich Sokolov-Skalia*, Moscow: Iskussto, 1940.

Lodder, C., *Constructive Strands in Russian Art 1914-1937*, London: The Pindar Press, 2005.

Misler, N., *Vasilii Kandinsky and the Russian Academy of Artistic Sciences,* Experiment vol. 8, Los Angeles, 2002, pp.173-185.
— *Vasilii Kandinsky at RAKhN*, Experiment, vol. 3, Los Angeles, 1997, pp. 148-156.

Pospelov, G.G., *Bubnovyi valet*, Moscow: Sovetskii khudozhnik, 1990.

Poushkarev, V., *Moi komandirovki v Parizh, Leonardo Benatov,* Nashe Nasledie/Our Heritage, Moscow, 47/1998, pp.35-49.

Rodchenko, A., *Experiments for the Future: Diaries, Essays, Letters and other writings*, edited by A. Lavrentiev, New York: The Museum of Modern Art, 2005.

Sophrony, Archimandrite, *Dukhovnye besedy*, tom 1 i 2, Moscow: Palomnik, 2003, 2007.

— *Eikodomontas ton Nao tou Theou,* 3 Volumes, Tolleshunt Knights: Stavropegic Monastery of Saint John the Baptist, 2013, 2014.

—*His Life is Mine*, Crestwood: St Vladimir's Seminary Press, 1988.

— *Letters to his Family*, Tolleshunt Knights: Stavropegic Monastery of St John the Baptist, 2015.

— *On Prayer*, Tolleshunt Knights: Stavropegic Monastery of St John the Baptist, 1996.

—*Rozhdenie v Tsarstvo nepokolbimoe*, Moscow: Palomnik, 2000.

— *Saint Silouan the Athonite*, Tolleshunt Knights: Stavropegic Monastery of Saint John the Baptist, 1991.

— *Striving for Knowledge of God*, Tolleshunt Knights: Stavropegic Monastery of St John the Baptist, 2016.

—*Tainstvo khristianskoi zhizni,* Sergiev Posad: Sviato-Troitskaia Lavra, 2009.

— *Truth and Life*, Tolleshunt Knights: Stavropegic Monastery of St John the Baptist, 2014.

— *We Shall See Him As He Is*, Tolleshunt Knights: Stavropegic Monastery of Saint John the Baptist, 1988.

— *Wisdom from Mount Athos*, Crestwood: St. Vladimir's Seminary Press, 1974.

Tsakiridou, C.A., *Icons in Time, Persons in Eternity*, Burlington: Ashgate, 2013.

Turchin, V.S., *Obrazy bytia, ili iskusstvo sozertsaniia*, Moscow: Libri di Arte, 2008.

Zacharias, Archimandrite, *Man, the Target of God*, Tolleshunt Knights: Stavropegic Monastery of St John the Baptist, 2015.

Weißback, A., *Kandinsky Unterricht am Bauhaus 1923-1233, Vorträge, Seminare, Übungen*, Berlin: Gebr. Mann verlag, 2015.

Acknowledgements

THIS WORK WOULD NOT have been possible without the assistance of many people to whom I am deeply indebted and grateful:

John E. Bowlt for invaluable help, encouragement and inspirational input.

My indefatigable and loyal editors and correctors: Napoleon Katsos, Nina Papadopoulos and Philippa Steer.

Linda Miller, Kasia Raczynski, Janice Wakeling, and the staff at Tiptree library for finding and supplying all essential material.

Anna Solovyova and Irina Krymova for helping to find source material in Russian archives and libraries.

Gennady Barabtarlo for translations at short notice.

Sebastian Brock, Nicoletta Misler, John Milner, Henry Milner, Christina Lodder, Aleksandr Aleksandras and others who prefer to stay anonymous for their generous assistance with all my questions.

Father Zacharias for his continual encouragement and support.

Printed in Dunstable, United Kingdom

70590949R00083